BLOWGUN
TECHNIQUES

THE DEFINITIVE GUIDE
TO MODERN AND TRADITIONAL
BLOWGUN TECHNIQUES

AMANTE P. MARIÑAS SR.
WITH A FOREWORD BY DR. HIRONORI HIGUCHI

TUTTLE PUBLISHING
Tokyo • Rutland, Vermont • Singapore

Published by Tuttle Publishing, an imprint of Periplus Editions (HK) Ltd., with editorial offices at 364 Innovation Drive, North Clarendon, Vermont 05759 U.S.A.

Library of Congress Cataloging-in-Publication Data

Marinas, Amante P.
  Blowgun techniques : the definitive guide to modern and traditional blowgun techniques / Amante P. Marinas ; with a foreword by Dr. Hironori Higuchi.
    p. cm.
  Includes bibliographical references.
  ISBN 978-0-8048-4013-2 (pbk.)
  1. Blowguns. I. Title.
  GN498.B5M37 2010   799.2028'2--dc22
                      2009046109

ISBN 978-0-8048-4013-2

Distributed by

North America, Latin America & Europe
Tuttle Publishing
364 Innovation Drive
North Clarendon, VT
05759-9436 U.S.A.
Tel: 1 (802) 773-8930
Fax: 1 (802) 773-6993
info@tuttlepublishing.com
www.tuttlepublishing.com

Japan
Tuttle Publishing
Yaekari Building, 3rd Floor
5-4-12 Osaki
Shinagawa-ku
Tokyo 141 0032
Tel: (81) 3 5437-0171
Fax: (81) 3 5437-0755
tuttle-sales@gol.com

Asia Pacific
Berkeley Books Pte. Ltd.
61 Tai Seng Avenue #02-12
Singapore 534167
Tel: (65) 6280-1330
Fax: (65) 6280-6290
inquiries@periplus.com.sg
www.periplus.com

14 13 12 11 10   10 9 8 7 6 5 4 3 2 1

Printed in Singapore

TABLE OF CONTENTS

DEDICATION

In loving memory of my father Virgilio

In loving memory of my brother Kuyang Pidiong

In loving memory of my mother Carolina

And to my brothers and sisters Milagros, Ernesto, Patricia, Remigia,
Pilar, Teodorico, Romulo, Wilhelmina, Manolo and Marissa

FOREWORD

The blowgun is still much in use at present by tropical jungle tribes but has long been forgotten as a weapon. It is a weak weapon but it offers something unique and different from other weapons that are used for hunting and for sport shooting.

Mr. Amante P. Mariñas Sr. recognized and studied the sports aspect of the blowgun and wrote the historical book *Pananandata Guide to Sport Blowguns* that was published in 1999 by United Cutlery Corp. In June 2001, in recognition of his work, I asked Mr. Mariñas to become the Co-Chairman of the International Sport Blowgun Association (ISBA) that I founded in October 1992. It was an honor for me when he accepted. The name ISBA had been changed in 2004 to International Fukiyado Association (IFA).

Mr. Mariñas and I have been promoting blowgun shooting as a sport. It is a sport that can be participated in by seniors, women, and the handicapped where they can become as good as stronger and healthier individuals. While the shooting of the blowgun may seem effortless, it still requires not only power, but also intelligence, total focus, and good technique.

If you have tried shooting the blowgun then you have experienced how absorbing and satisfying it is and how it can lead to hours of fun. I hope that you would experience the health effect of the sport and would introduce the sport to your friends. Shooting the blowgun is an enjoyable and a beneficial activity to engage in.

Mr. Mariñas, a chemical engineer, has applied his science background to do an in-depth study of the shooting of the blowgun. He has practiced blow gunning for many years. It is amazing that he has shot the blowgun more than 700,000 times to gather the information he needed to find the answers to questions he had asked himself.

This work will lead you to a better understanding of the blowgun and will teach you the uniqueness of and the fine techniques needed to attain a high level of skill in the sport. This must be the textbook of blowgun for beginners and should be read by all blowgun shooters.

Hironori Higuchi, MD
Nagaoka, Japan, IFA Co-Chairman

PREFACE

Our house was surrounded by trees, mostly fruit-bearing, such as *mango, guava, atis, guyabano, kamatsile, saresa, balubad* and *bignay*. They would shed their leaves once a year at which time my mother would use the *walis na tingting*.

To the left of my house were two kapok trees. To the right of my house, reachable from our open porch is achiote. A few feet away from the achiote are banana plants. To the back of the house was our bamboo grove.

Thus, I had all that was needed to make a blowgun—bamboo for the barrel and for the dart, walis na tingting for the dart, kapok to feather and achiote to color my darts and a ready made soft target: banana trunks.

But the sumpit, the blowgun that I made, served only as a toy.

I now live in Fredericksburg, Virginia half a world away from Pambuan, a small village in Central Luzon in the Philippines where I grew up.

I still shoot blowguns. But the blowguns and the darts that I now shoot, I buy from mail order houses.

ACKNOWLEDGMENTS

I would like to thank: **Marty Bohanon** for the camouflage, 3-piece .40 caliber blowgun. **Bruce Bell** for the list of ASBA affiliated associations. **Jose Capitulo** for posing as an attacker. **Steve Charlson** for the curtain rods and a .40 caliber blowgun. **Fred Cupolo** for posing as an attacker. **Joseph Darrah** for the .50 caliber blowgun. **Ueli Laeng** for the bahi and yantok blowguns and the blowgun rack. **Robert Mulligan** for taking the photographs in Chapter 14. **David Paiva** for the Cherokee blowgun and the Peruvian pucuna. **Peter Sampogna** for posing as an attacker. **Tracy and Larry Schnitzer** for the bamboo blowguns. **Dave Sustak** for the chronological history of the sport of blowgun shooting. **Lynn Thompson**, president of Cold Steel, for the .625 caliber blowgun. **Greg Vecchi** for the landscape timber and the 2" by 4"s. **Dr. Hironori Higuchi** for writing the Foreword, for the .51 caliber blowgun and fukiya darts. **Thoraya Zedan** for taking all the other photographs, for two laptop computers and for solving all my computer problems. Especial thanks to my wife **Cherry** and son **Mat Jr.** for giving me all the time I needed to complete this work.

WARNING

Blowguns are not toys and safety must be your first concern when you practice shooting the blowgun.

Darts—especially those with sharp tips—are very dangerous and may cause injury if misused or carelessly handled.

Adult supervision and adequate training is recommended when the blowgun is used by a minor for their safety and for those of others in the area.

You must conform to all laws concerning the ownership and use of blowguns and assume all responsibility of all safety practices and legal use.

chapter 1

TRADITIONAL BLOWGUNS

The blowgun is essentially a long, hollow tube through which projectiles such as darts or pellets are shot. The projectiles are propelled by a blast of air from the user's lungs. Blowguns are designed to deliver darts from a distance—silently. They have been used by many cultures either for hunting small game or for sporting.

Traditional blowguns were handcrafted and were constructed of materials native to the shooter.

INDONESIAN, MALAYSIAN AND PHILIPPINE BLOWGUNS

The traditional Philippine blowgun is called *sumpit* but was given the name *zarbatana* by the Spaniards. The word is a variant of *cerbatana*, a lance. The Indonesian blowgun is called *sumpitan*. In the village where I grew up we made *sumpits*, toy blowguns, from short straight sections of bamboo. Note that the Brazilian blowgun is called *zarabatana*[1] indicating a common origin of the word.

Blowguns from Indonesia, Malaysia and the Philippines are usually made from bamboo. However, occasionally, one would find blowguns made from hardwood. Blowguns double as hand held-clubs or spears when darts run out.

Straight sections of bamboo are needed to make the blowguns. Bamboo, if crooked can be straightened by heating it over a fire. The bamboo is first sprayed with water to prevent

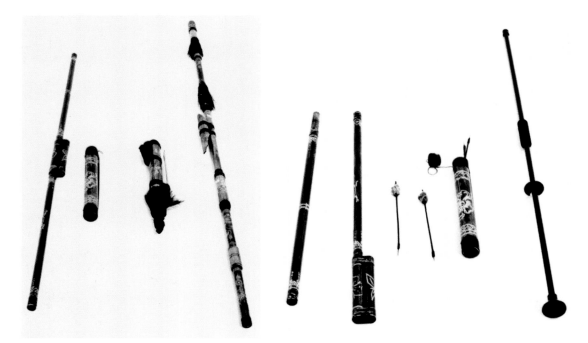

FIGURE 1-1. Bamboo blowguns. two-piece and three-piece blowguns and quivers (left); a disassembled two-piece blowgun (right). Poison for the darts used in the sumpit was taken from the tree called *quemandag*; for the sumpitan, from the *upas* tree.

it from charring. The crooked part of the bamboo is rotated over the fire to ensure that it becomes uniformly flexible. The bamboo then is pressed against a tree trunk to straighten the crooked part. The crooked part can also be pressed against the knee to straighten it. If the bamboo bends again, the process is repeated until it is straight. It is then allowed to dry.

The bamboo blowgun can be one-piece and is usually about 4 feet. It is this short because it is not easy to remove the barriers from longer pieces of bamboo. The barriers are removed by hammering on a small diameter piece of hardwood to the end of which is attached a small metal point. The barriers are smoothed using an arc-shaped sharp metal piece that is attached to the end of a long piece of hardwood.

It is easier to remove and smooth the inside of shorter sections of bamboo. It is also easier to find short sections of bamboo that are straight. Thus, two-piece or three-piece blowguns can be made from bamboo with couplings (also made from bamboo) used to connect the short sections.

The shafts for the darts are also made from bamboo. Short pieces of bamboo are cut between two nodes and then split into smaller thin pieces. The shafts are then rounded to the required diameter using knives or broken bottles. The shafts are between 6 to 10 inches long.

The shaft can also be made from the *walis tingting* (a broom) that is made from the spine of the leaves of a palm tree. The walis tinting was used to sweep leaves around our house in our yard in the village where I grew up.

The shafts are feathered with the yellowish cotton-like material taken from the pod of the kapok tree. The blunt end of the shaft is first rubbed with a sticky resin. The kapok sticks to the resin and is then wrapped around the shaft into the shape of the modern q-tip.[2] The sharp tip is fire-hardened.

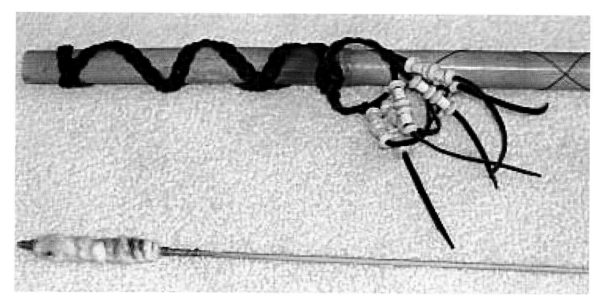

FIGURE 1-2. A Cherokee blowgun made from river cane and its dart.

CHEROKEE BLOWGUNS

The Cherokee blowgun is made from river cane a species of bamboo that is native to and grows well in the southeastern US. Indeed, where I live in Fredericksburg, Virginia, one will see river cane growing by the roadside.

The Cherokees make their blowguns from straight sections of river cane. Ideal lengths are 6-8 foot straight sections. River cane of the proper length can be straightened by heating any crooked portion over a fire. The river cane is then bent the opposite way and held in the position to prevent it from bending back. It is then sun-dried for several days. The Cherokee blowgun is made in two ways:

- Embers are dropped on the barriers to burn them. An arrow attached to a small stick further removes the barriers and smoothes the inside. To finish the blowgun, a smaller diameter river cane is inserted into the blowgun to rub the inside.

- The river cane is split down its length into halves to get at the barriers. The barriers are then scraped with a knife and then smoothed. The long sections are then glued together and lashed with sinew.

The shaft for the dart for use with the blowgun is made from any hardwood such as black locust. The dart is traditionally between 18-20 inches long and is feathered with thistle down. Thistle is best picked during August. Thistle down is wrapped around the shaft's dull end then tied with sinew.

The Cherokee darts were never poisoned because they were used for hunting small game for food.

SOUTH AMERICAN BLOWGUNS

ECUADORIAN BLOWGUN– The Waoranis of Ecuador use the knot-free *chonta* tree to make blowguns that are at least 9½ feet long. They cut a sapling and split it down the middle to expose the soft core.

It takes several days for the Waorani to make the blowgun. He has first to remove the soft core and carefully carve the center into half cylinders. The two halves are then tied securely with vine. The inside of the blowgun is smoothed by repeatedly pouring sand into it. The final polish is done by rubbing the inside with a wooden rod and then running fine clay through the bore. The outside of the finished blowgun is elliptical. Thus shaped, it will fit across the mouth in much the same way as the mouthpiece of the .625 caliber blowgun (Figure 2-6, right) does.

The Waoranis as well as the Capahuaris of Ecuador fashion darts from the spine of the leaves of the *maximiliana regia* palm tree and fletches their darts with kapok. The darts are poisoned with curare for use on the woolly monkeys, toucans, and on the nocturnal *currasow* that they hunt for food.

PERUVIAN BLOWGUN– The best known Peruvian *pucunas* (blowgun) is made by the *Yaqua* tribe. The Yaquas use the blowguns for hunting monkeys, birds, and other small animals such as the sloth.

The pucuna is 6 to 7 feet long and is made from *pucuna caspi* (blowgun wood). The bore is chiseled out on two matching halves then tied together with a cord made from the *chambira* palm. The bore is rough-smoothed using a rod made from the *pona* palm with the final polish made by passing fine sand repeatedly through the bore.

FIGURE 1-3. The Waorani blowgun has an elliptical cross-section that fits the shape of the mouth, is at least 9 feet long, and has a bore of about ½ inch.

The assembled blowgun is wrapped with the skin of the *huambe* vine. For a smooth feel, the skin is wrapped inside out and glued to the blowgun with resin from the copal plant. The wrapping is stained black.

The darts are made from the ribs of the *maximiliana regia* palm tree fletched with kapok and are carried in a basket-like quiver called the *cargajo*. The kapok is carried in a nut from which the inside was removed. The dart is dipped in poison the main component of which is curare. The composition of the poison is a well-guarded secret.

FIGURE 1-4. Peruvian pucuna.

FIGURE 1-5. The spool-like mouthpiece is made from wood.

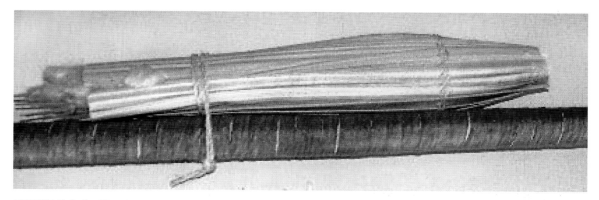

FIGURE 1-6. The *birutas* (darts) are carried in the basket-like cargajo that is made from the leaves of the *catirina* palm tree.

CHINESE BLOWGUNS

One of two blowguns used by ancient Chinese martial arts masters is called the *mea hua needle.* It is tiny being only 2 inches long and is made from goose feathers. It is believed that a woman first used it because the shaft of the dart is a 1½ inch sewing needle. The dart is feathered with flannel.

FIGURE 1-7. The quiver can also be made from bamboo. The kapok is stored in a nut and pulled out to fletch a dart. The blowgun is coated with a black stain taken from the *cumaca* tree.

One other blowgun created during the Yuan Dynasty is called the *blowing arrow*. It is made from a short section of bamboo that is about 6 inches long. The blowgun shoots a 5-inch dart with a bamboo shaft that is tipped with a metal point.

In the Chinese martial arts, both blowguns are considered hidden weapons.

JAPANESE BLOWGUNS

The Japanese blowgun is called *fukiya*. The traditional dart is called *fukidari* and is 2 inches long.

The ninja book *Mansenshukai* written in the Edo era about 200 years ago shows a picture of a paper blowgun dart. The Japanese novelist Saikaku Ebara, in 1688, wrote that the blowgun was popular at the time.

The website of Dr. Hironori Higuchi showed a 254 cm blowgun said to weigh about 2 kg that was made 130 years ago. However, there is no mention of how the blowgun was made and what type of wood (or metal) was used to make it.

Strangely enough, though bamboo also grows in Japan, there was no mention of it being used to make blowguns.

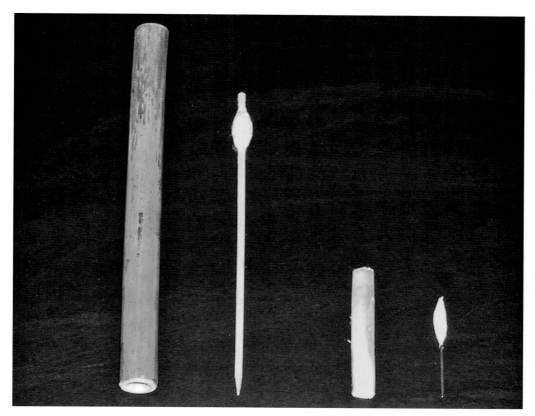

FIGURE 1-8. The 6-inch blowing arrow and the 2-inch mea hua needle.

FIGURE 1-9. A Japanese fukiya
(A rendering from a sketch in the IFA website).

chapter 2

MODERN
BLOWGUNS

Modern blowguns are made from heat-tempered, precision seamless aluminum. Thus, the barrel is relatively light and will not rust. The modern blowgun is provided with a mouthpiece and shoots darts with plastic tails and steel or bamboo shafts.

BARREL

Modern blowguns can be one-piece, two-piece or three-piece. The latter two can be assembled and disassembled in minutes. The short sections are connected to each other with plastic couplings.

Take-down blowguns are designed for easy carrying to the target site. A one-piece, 5-foot blowgun will be difficult to transport.

Some modern blowguns are also designed as walking canes (Figure 2-5).

MOUTHPIECE

The modern blowgun features a mouthpiece (Figure 2-5, Figure 2-6). Most traditional blowguns do not have mouthpieces. The mouthpiece allows the focusing of the blown air into the launching of the dart. Thus, there is little wasted air.

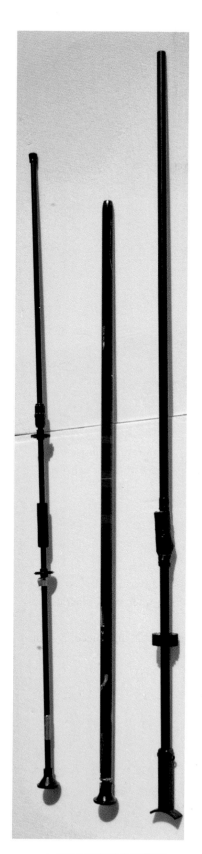

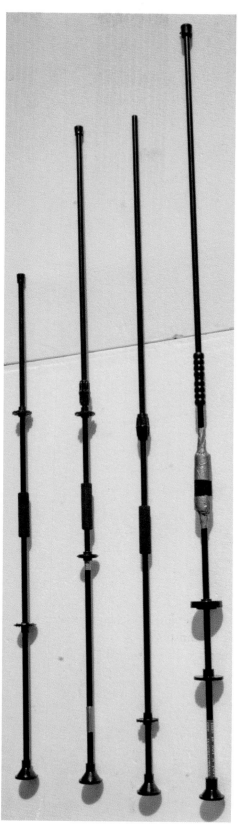

FIGURE 2-1 (far left).
Modern one-piece blowguns
(left to right):
.40 caliber (4 feet 6 inches),
.50 caliber (4 feet),
.625 caliber (5 feet)

FIGURE 2-2 (left).
.40 caliber blowguns of different lengths:
one-piece 3 feet 6inches (left); two-piece 4 feet 5 inches (middle two);
two-piece 5 feet (right)

FIGURE 2-3 (right).
A .40 caliber, three-piece, 60 inches camouflage blowgun where the sections are joined via sleeves. A black rubber tube is slipped over the sleeves to secure the connections.

FIGURE 2-4 (middle).
A Japanese three-piece, .51 caliber (13 mm), 4½ feet aluminum blowgun that uses rolled plastic sheet as coupling (left).

FIGURE 2-5 (far right).
The one-piece, .50 caliber blowgun shown in Figure 2-1, is also designed for use as a walking cane. The funnel-like mouthpiece made from wood serves as the grip on the cane (bottom, left). The cane is provided with a drawer knob-like piece (top, left) that is inserted at the muzzle. The stem of the drawer knob is encased in cork. (A good friend of mine, David Paiva encased the aluminum tube in wood that was in turn hand painted by his wife, Hannah.)

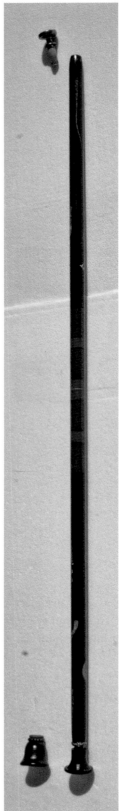

FIGURE 2-6. Mouthpieces of commercial blowguns: a .40 (left) and a .50 caliber blowgun (middle) with funnel mouthpieces; a .625 blowgun (right) with a mouthpiece that is radically different. The white tape helps to orient the blowgun the same way for each shot.

The mouthpiece, made of plastic, is a molded one-piece construction with safety rings to prevent inhaling the dart. There is no such provision in the traditional blowguns. Hence, the traditional blowguns required more skill in its use considering that they were oftentimes aimed at targets overhead. Thus, there is greater risk of inhaling a dart when shooting a traditional blowgun.

The mouthpiece is not necessary when you only shoot occasionally. There will be little harm if your teeth or lips touch an aluminum or bamboo tube. However, if you shoot a couple of hundred darts a day, you need to use a mouthpiece.

In my case, I shot the .51 caliber blowgun without a mouthpiece. However after shooting 200 darts a day for 5 days, I felt indentations in my lower and upper lip. So I made a mouthpiece for it.

You will not feel comfortable shooting a .625 caliber blowgun with no mouthpiece. It is just too big for the mouth.

PROJECTILES

The tail of the commercial dart can be either a cone or a spherical bead (Figure 2-7). The cone darts come with sharp or broad head point shafts or with plastic broad heads.

FIGURE 2-7. Bead (left) and cone (middle) tails used on a .40 caliber blowgun and on a .50 caliber blowgun (right). The darts have to be assembled.

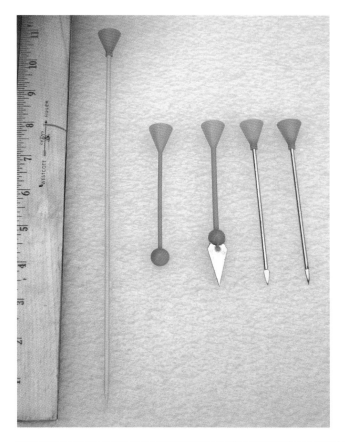

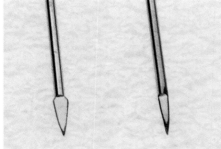

FIGURE 2-8. Darts for use with the .625 Magnum blowgun. The dart which is second from right is the original dart but I grounded the point to remove the flare (extreme right) because it was not easy pulling it out from the cardboard target. The darts come assembled. The dart third from left, because it has a broad head, sometimes will not shoot straight, particularly on a windy day. One other contributing factor to its erratic trajectory is the two fin-like protuberances on the ball where the tip is mounted.

Commercial darts can have cone tails that are white, orange, green, blue, red, or yellow. The flange of the cone is constructed such that it collapses when pushed through the mouthpiece past the safety ring. As soon as the dart clears the mouthpiece into the barrel, the cone returns to its original shape. With this feature, the possibility of inhaling such a dart is unlikely.

The darts of .40 caliber blowguns have 4-inch steel shafts that have to be inserted into plastic cones or beads. The darts of .50 caliber blowguns have 3½-inch shafts. The shafts of the .625 caliber darts are 4 inches long.

Modern blowguns can also be loaded with paintballs—thin nylon coated balls that break upon impact, releasing a water-soluble dye.

QUIVER

Most modern blowguns are provided with quivers that are attached to the barrel. The quivers can hold ten or eight darts (Figure 2-9).

FOAM GRIP

Most blowguns are provided with a foam grip for comfort and for protection against the cold of winter (Figure 2-9). The placement of the grip will depend on the length of the shooter's arm.

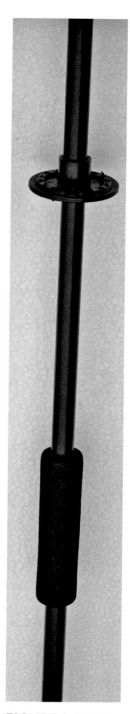

FIGURE 2-9. The foam grip and the quiver on the blowgun.

chapter 3

MAKING YOUR OWN BLOWGUN

You can make your own blowgun from readily available materials. Whether it will cost more or less than a commercially sold blowgun will depend on the equipment you now have. It will definitely cost more than a commercial blowgun should you decide to buy the tools needed to make one.

A blowgun is essentially a barrel, a tube, or a pipe. Hence, pipes made of plastic or of metal such as copper, aluminum, or steel are, in a way, ready made blowguns.
Wood, solid or hollow, can be fashioned into a blowgun.

WOOD

If you have access to the *chonta* tree like the Ecuadorians do, cut a sapling, split it along its length, then carve half cylinders in each. Smooth and then tie the split sections together with vine and give a final polish to the tube by passing sand and then clay through the bore repeatedly.

Yantok (rattan), also solid wood, has the desired circular cross section that decreases in diameter toward the top. Rattan comes relatively straight and is very flexible. Indeed, small diameter rattans can be straightened against the knee. It has continuous fibers and would normally fray instead of breaking clean. Straight short sections can be cut from long rattan poles.

To make the blowgun, the rattan pole is first cut in half lengthwise then semi-cylindrical grooves running through its length are cut out with a router (Figure 3-1). To complete the blowgun, the two halves are glued together then bound with twine. Excess glue is removed by running a small piece of sponge repeatedly through the bore.

Anahaw is a hard wood while rattan is very porous. Anahaw is difficult to work with (Figure 3-2). Normally rattan will not be but it will also be very difficult to fashion into a blowgun unless you have the necessary equipment and skill.

Wood will swell when it comes in contact with water. In the anahaw, this is barely noticeable because it is dark brown. The swelling of rattan fibers will be visible. For this reason, lacquer has to be applied to the half cylindrical grooves. To ensure the smooth travel of the dart, the bore will have to be sprayed with a lubricant.

Kawayan (bamboo) has a natural hollow. To make a blowgun from bamboo, use the straightest bamboo you can find and also one with the least taper. If the bamboo is slightly bent, use wet steam to soften it then straighten it against your knee. Apply gentle pressure. Otherwise, you will break the pole. Do not put a steamed bamboo against your bare skin!

Cut the desired blowgun length then split the bamboo down its length using a machete like a wedge to expose the barriers. Remove the barriers with a whittling knife then rough smooth with a round file. Use coarse then fine sandpaper to smooth the barrier.

Bamboo has a thin translucent film of paper-like material in its inside. Applying gentle pressure, remove the thin film with fine sandpaper.

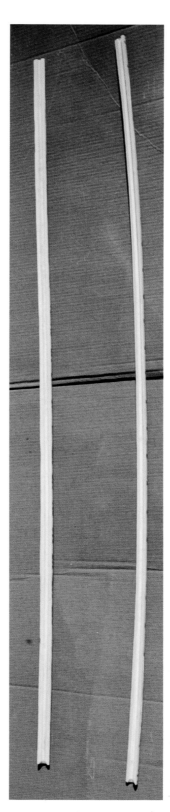

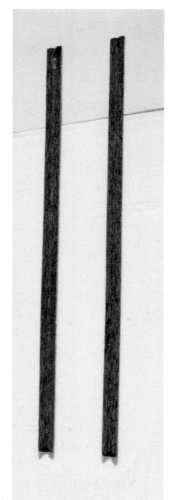

FIGURE 3-1 (left). Two halves of a 60-inch rattan pole to be later glued together into a blowgun. Darts will be loaded through the conical-shaped end that will serve as the mouthpiece.

FIGURE 3-2 (above). Two halves of a 30-inch length of anahaw prior to assembly. Darts will be loaded through the conical-shaped end that will serve as the mouthpiece.

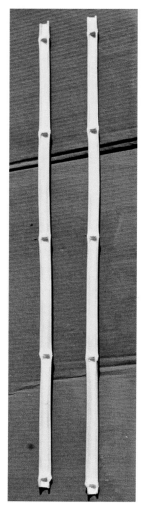

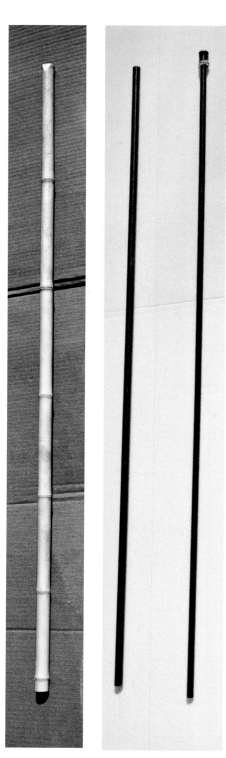

FIGURE 3-3 (above). Two halves of a split 34½-inch bamboo pole with the barriers that have to be removed.

FIGURE 3-4 (center). A 46-inch, one-piece, un-split, .50 caliber blowgun I made from river cane.

FIGURE 3-5 (right). Blowguns made from 48-inch steel curtain rods.

One need not split river cane to make a blowgun. I made one by using a sharpened solid steel rod to break the barriers (Figure 3-4). I smoothed the barriers using a curtain rod that I beveled at its end. I am able to shoot the long plastic .51 caliber fukiya darts through it.

METAL

Aluminum, steel, brass, or even copper tubing can be used as the barrel of a blowgun. All you need to do is find the right bore and obtain the right length of material.

Sometimes, a blowgun barrel can come from an unlikely source.

I teach stick fighting in my backyard. In one training session, one of my students gave me two 4-foot long steel pipes one inside the other. It was a curtain rod that was lightly rusted at both ends as well as on the inside.

I cleaned the bore with steel wool then beveled both ends with a conical grindstone to ensure that the dart exits unimpeded. The tubes were not seamless but I smoothed them as best I could and then sprayed the bore with lubricant.

The inner tube happened to have a .40 caliber bore (Figure 3-5). I was able to borrow the mouthpiece and the muzzle cover from one of my shorter commercial blowguns and put them on the curtain rod. I was able to shoot the commercial .40 caliber darts and tails made from a ³⁄₈-inch dowel through the rod.

The outer tube of the curtain rod has an inside diameter of about ¹⁄₂-inch. I fitted it with a mouthpiece. I am able to shoot homemade darts with tails made from a ¹⁄₂-inch dowel through it.

PVC

A 5-foot long, schedule 40, ¹⁄₂-inch PVC pipe costs about $1.00. A funnel fashioned into a mouth-piece will cost about 50 cents. Hence for less than $2.00, you can make a high caliber blowgun. It will cost even less if you fashion the mouthpiece from a plastic soft drink bottle.

PVC pipes come with different wall thickness. For example: A schedule 40, ¹⁄₂-inch PVC pipe has a ¹⁄₈-inch wall thickness. Another PVC pipe I made into a blowgun has a ¹⁄₂-inch outside diam-eter and a thin wall.

A thin-walled PVC pipe will sag due to its own weight. However, a 5-foot long schedule 40 PVC pipe is rigid enough to shoot straight. To keep the PVC pipe straight, place it inside a bamboo tube from which the barriers were removed. In addition to keeping the pipe straight, the bamboo tube will camouflage it and even protect it during transport.

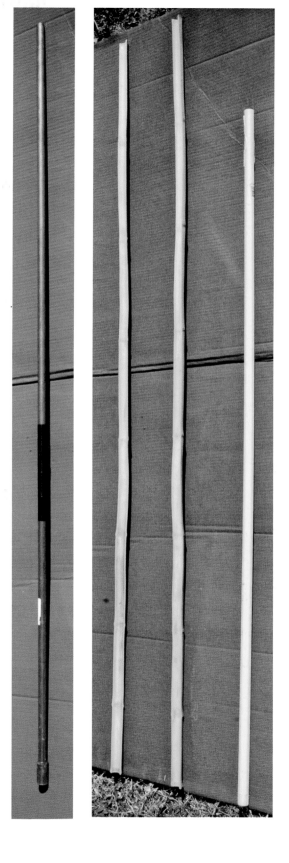

FIGURE 3-6 (right). A 5-foot blowgun made from copper tubing. The black duct tape provides a warm handle during cold days.

FIGURE 3-7 (far right). A blowgun made from a 60-inch PVC pipe. The PVC pipe will sag. To keep the pipe straight, it can be inserted between two halves of a bamboo pole (left) from which the barri-ers are removed.

MOUTHPIECE

A mouthpiece is essentially a funnel, an inverted cone, with a hole at the small end leading into a tapering or cylindrical tube (stem). The mouthpiece centers the flow of air into the barrel. The commercial mouthpiece is typically about 1½-inch across and ½-inch deep. The stem is ⅝-inch long.

The mouthpiece can be fashioned from the necks of plastic containers.

FUNNELS. A three-piece pack of funnels I bought cost $2.19. After a shop discount, each funnel cost me about 50 cents.

To make the mouthpiece,
- Mark the funnel about 1½" from its narrow opening.
- Place the funnel on a flat surface.
- Hold the funnel with your left hand and cut it on a plane parallel to the flat surface using a thin saw.
- Rough-smooth the cut edge on a disk sander or rub it on sandpaper laid flat on a table.
- Check the fit in your mouth. Remove material as necessary.
- Smooth the edges with fine sandpaper.
- Insert the pipe into the stem of the funnel.
- Remove material as necessary.

If you want to fix the funnel to the pipe, apply glue inside the stem then insert the pipe. Make sure to remove excess glue. However, if you shoot in the field, it will be easier to transport a blowgun without its mouthpiece. In this case, do not glue the funnel to the barrel. When you shoot, attach the funnel to the barrel. When you finish shooting, pull it out.

FIGURE 3-8. Two cuts to make a mouthpiece from a funnel.

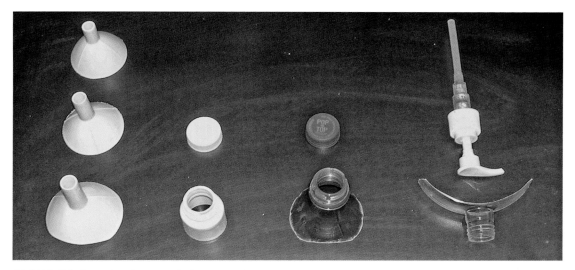

FIGURE 3-9. Mouthpieces (left to right): fashioned from funnels, a pill container, and a soft drink bottle. At extreme right is a mouthpiece made from the neck of a hand sanitizer dispenser that is similar to the mouthpiece on the .625 caliber Magnum blowgun.

PLASTIC PILL CONTAINERS OR SOFT DRINKS BOTTLES. Pill containers or the neck of a soft drink plastic bottle can be fashioned into mouthpieces. You can even contour the mouthpiece to fit your cheeks. You might need to wrap several layers of electrical tape around the pipe to increase its diameter to fit the mouthpiece.

GRIP

The outside diameter of a .40 caliber commercial blowgun is about ½-inch which is too small for a shooter who has big hands. For this reason, most commercial blowguns are provided with a foam grip. The grip will allow a secure and comfortable hold on the blowgun and will

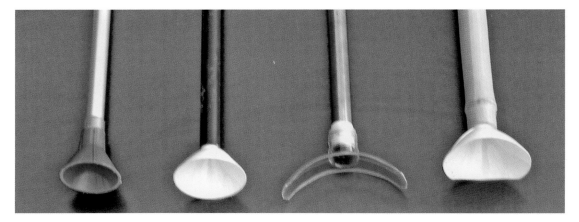

FIGURE 3-10. Homemade mouthpieces (left to right) fitted on aluminum, steel, copper, and bamboo blowguns.

prevent your hand from freezing onto the barrel should you decide to shoot your blowgun during winter.

The .625 caliber Magnum blowgun is not provided with a foam grip. However, you can wrap foam around the barrel then duct tape it to form a grip. You might be able to find a discarded garden hose that could fit the outside diameter of the barrel or bamboo with the right inside diameter to fit your blowgun.

MUZZLE PROTECTOR

The blowgun needs little maintenance. However, if you are to shoot with consistent accuracy, it has to be kept in good condition.

Commercial blowguns are provided with plastic muzzle caps that prevent the aluminum pipe from getting dented. A homemade blowgun can be protected in the same way.

A number of materials can be used to protect the muzzle of your blowgun. You can use any short length tube of rubber, plastic, or wood. The muzzle protector should extend about 1/2-inch past the lip of the muzzle, must be rigid, and must not interfere with the smooth exit of the dart.

A short length of bamboo (tube) can be used as a muzzle protector. The bamboo tube has to be constructed such that it cannot slide too far in and expose the tip of the muzzle to possible damage. To imitate the construction of the commercial muzzle protector, use a conical grinding stone to enlarge the bore of the bamboo tube at one end.

COUPLING

A long blowgun can be made from several short lengths of pipe. This will allow you to have a long-barreled blowgun that can be assembled and disassembled in the field, thus making transport less difficult.

FIGURE 3-11. Grips: a homemade foam grip (right) with duct tape wrapped around it and a commercial foam grip (far right).

Ease of transport is not the only reason for a takedown version. A takedown version is also required should you use PVC pipes to make a blowgun. Long pipes made of PVC will bend due to weight. To make a blowgun of the desired length from PVC, you will need two or three short pieces which you can join using a coupling.

A coupling can be metal or wood with an inside diameter that matches the outside diameters of short tube sections. It is used to connect two short tubes to make one long tube. Where the two tubes meet the joint must be seamless or nearly so to ensure the smooth travel of the dart.

Commercial two-piece blowguns come with plastic couplings. You can make a three-piece blowgun from two two-piece blowguns. In this way you can make a 7-foot blowgun that you can assemble and disassemble in the field. However, such a 7-foot blowgun will have an unavoidable curve. Despite the curve, with some practice, you can still have a good shooting average.

A coupling need not be made of metal. For example: Indonesian, Malaysian, and Philippine two- and three-piece bamboo blowguns (Figure 1-1) use bamboo with a bigger diameter as coupling. The two-piece bamboo blowgun has one piece measuring 25½ inches and the other 27½ inches but with the overlap its overall length comes to 49½ inches. The three-piece blowgun consists of three 22½" sections that give the blowgun an overall length of 62 inches.

Blowgun master Dr. Hironori Higuchi uses couplings made from rolled plastic films (Figure 3-13) on three-section aluminum blowguns. The coupling can easily be slipped over the aluminum tube. A "quick and dirty" coupling using the same idea can be made from thicker-than-usual paper.

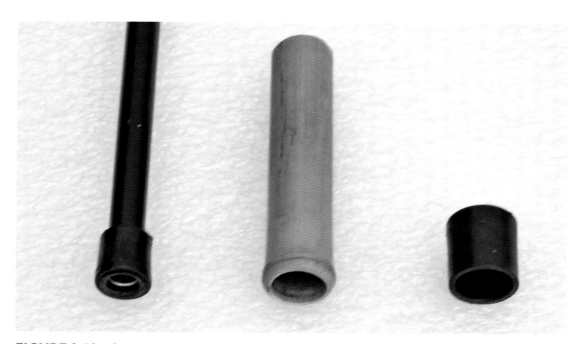

FIGURE 3-12. Commercial blowgun with a muzzle protector attached (left) and a protector made from bamboo (middle). The muzzle protector at extreme right encloses the muzzle.

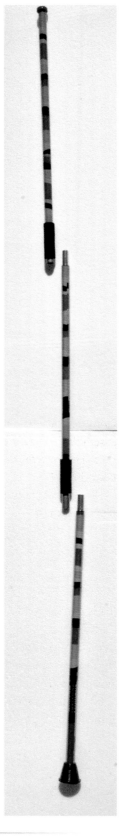

FIGURE 3-13 (top right). Couplings (left to right) made from copper, plastic film, and bamboo.

FIGURE 3-14 (bottom right and right). Sleeves. This three-piece .40 caliber camouflage commercial blowgun does not use a coupling. Each section simply slips into the other. When assembled it has a total length of 60 inches.

chapter 4

MAKING YOUR OWN DARTS

Commercial .40 and .50 caliber darts come unassembled. The .625 Magnum darts come assembled. Their tails will not last indefinitely. Their collapsible flanges will eventually rupture. Hence, you will end up with shafts with no tails. You can save the shafts to make your own darts.

Darts can be homemade in as little as 15 minutes even if you have to make the tail separate from the shaft.

TAIL

Tails can be made from wood, cotton, kapok, paper, aluminum, or plastic sheets.

WOOD. Wood such as dowels, cork from champagne bottles, or small branches of trees can be made into tails. Young rattans that are almost perfectly cylindrical can be obtained, though with some difficulty, from companies in the US that sell rattan as well as bamboo.

A $\frac{3}{8}$-inch dowel made from poplar costs less than a dollar and will fit a .40 caliber blowgun. A $\frac{7}{16}$-inch dowel will fit a $\frac{1}{2}$-inch PVC pipe. To make a tail from any dowel

- Mark the center of the dowel.
- Drill the hole for the shaft.
- Shape this end into a bullet nose to minimize wind resistance.

- Cut 1-inch long cylinders then mark the center.
- Hollow out this end using a conical grinding stone.

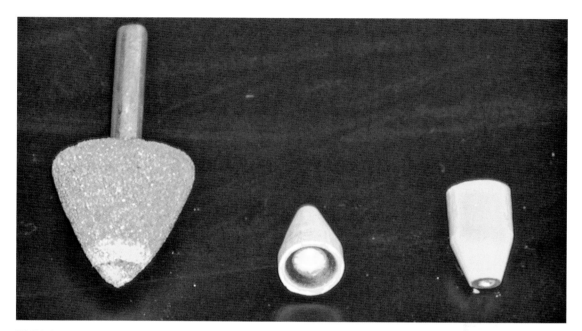

FIGURE 4-1. Bullet-nosed wooden tail with hollowed out back ends. The hollow is made with a conical grinding stone.

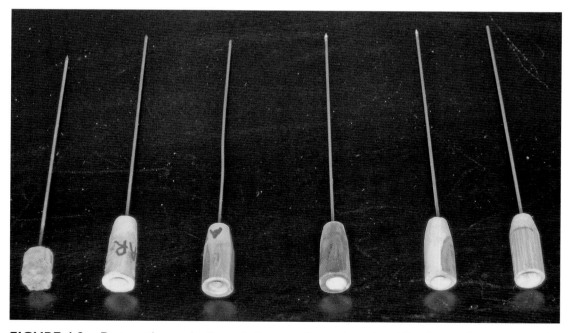

FIGURE 4-2. Darts with wood tails made from small tree branches. The dart at the extreme left is tailed with cork.

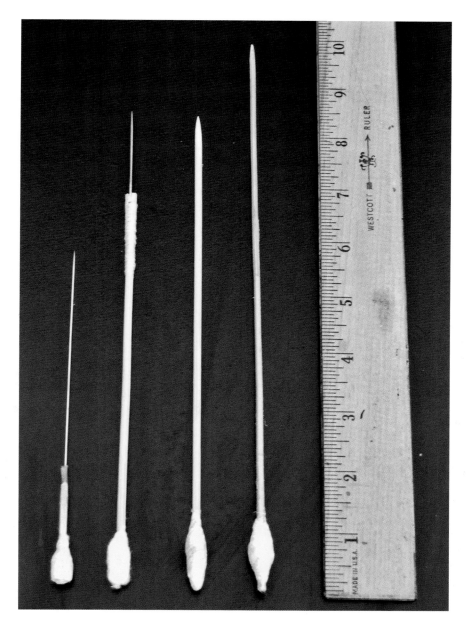

FIGURE 4-3. Darts feathered with cotton (left to right): a tail made from half of a q-tip with a shaft made from a doll needle, a bamboo shaft tipped with a sewing needle, an all-bamboo shaft, and a shaft from the stem of a leaf of the *maximiliana regia* palm tree. This is the same type of dart that the Ecuadoreans use in their blowguns.

Champagne bottles are a good source of corks from which you can make tails. You can also find corks of assorted sizes in arts and crafts shops. You can rough shape the cork with a razor blade then smooth it with sandpaper.

COTTON AND KAPOK. The yellowish "cotton" from the kapok tree is more readily available in the tropics.

Cotton or kapok can be easily shaped to fit the bore of any blowgun. Use a small amount of glue to attach the cotton to the shaft. To shape the tail, hold the cotton with your left hand and rotate the shaft with your right hand. Apply a small amount of glue as you wrap the cotton on top of another layer. You will end up with a tail shaped like a big q-tip. To make the tail retain its shape longer, lightly spray the tail with varnish.

You can get cotton rounds (circular flat, thin) from pharmacies. Cut ½-inch strips. Place the glue and then wrap the strip around the tail. Apply a small amount of glue on the strip as you wrap it to prevent the cotton from unraveling. You can use the same procedure on napkins. However, because the resulting tail is porous and cylindrical, air resistance will be substantial. Such darts will only be accurate when shot from short distances—from about 15 feet.

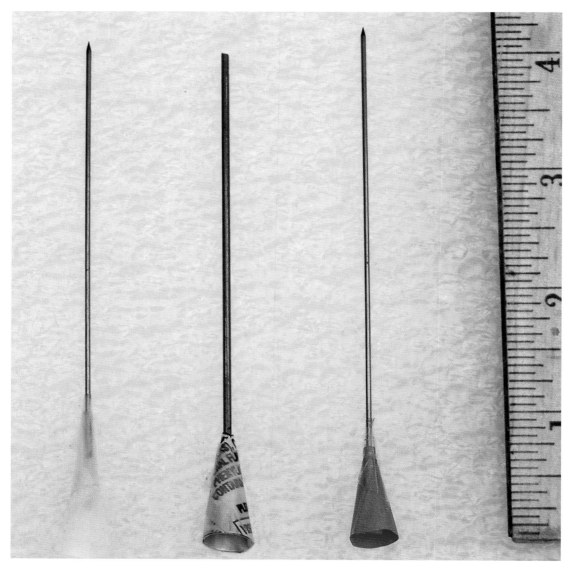

FIGURE 4-4. Darts (left to right) with tails made from plastic film, an aluminum sheet from a soda can, and paper.

PLASTIC FILM, PAPER, AND ALUMINUM SHEETS. Thicker-than-usual print paper, aluminum sheets from soda cans, or plastic films can be shaped into cones (Figure 4-4). Such cones will be hollow and will catch the full blast of air.

Form a cone using a strip of material that is at least 1½ inches wide and 2½ inches long. Insert the shaft through the cone then tape the front end of the cone to the shaft. Drop the cone at the muzzle end of the blowgun. Mark at the point of contact. Cut at the mark and

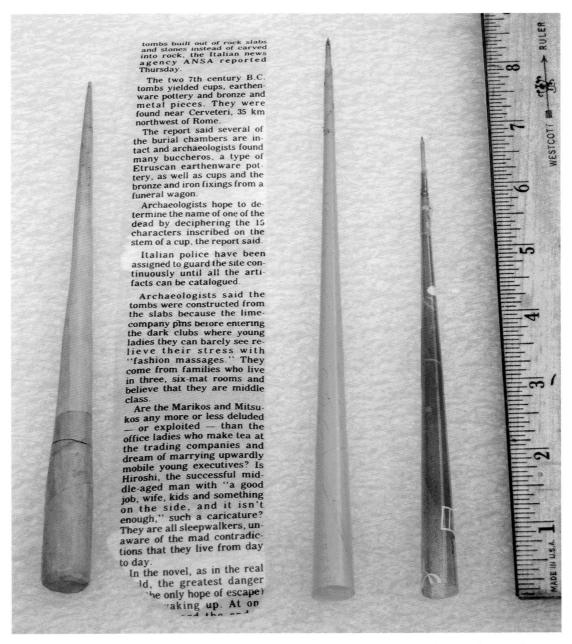

FIGURE 4-5. The Japanese fukiya dart (second from right) has an 8-inch tail made from a thin plastic film (second from left) that is shaped into a cone with the help of the conical piece of wood shown at extreme left.

trim as necessary. The adhesive tape will hold the cone in place during loading, in flight, and at impact. Make sure that the adhesive tape is wrapped smoothly to minimize air resistance.

If your blowgun has a mouthpiece, you might have to muzzle-load your homemade dart. Hence, the diameter of the cone should be just a shade smaller than the bore of your blowgun. Despite this, you will still have a good seal. Blown air will cause the cone to expand, thus assuring a good fit.

You can make paper cones from brightly colored stick pads. Use red or orange paper. Yellow or white paper can hardly be seen from 30 feet. (You need to see where your previous dart hits in case you need to correct your aim.) You can waterproof the paper by spraying or brushing lightly with varnish before forming the cone.

A very unique tail that is popular in Japan is made from a 9-inch by 2-inch thin plastic film. The cone is about 8 $\frac{1}{16}$ inches long through which end is inserted a short nail. Only about $\frac{1}{16}$-inch of the sharp tip is exposed and forms the shaft (Figure 4-5). It is an ingenious design for sport shooting.

READY MADE PLASTIC CONES AND BEADS. There is a good chance that you have ready-made cones at home that you are about to throw away such as empty medicine bottles or ball pens that refuse to write. If you are about to get rid of a Venetian blind, remove the cones from its twines and use them as tails.

Caps of small medicine bottles or eye-drop containers are almost always conical. You need only about fifteen minutes using a belt sander to trim it to the bore of your blowgun. However, you still have to center-drill a hole in it. Or punch a hole through it using a nail.

In some ball pen types, conical portions can be unscrewed (or sawed) then trimmed to fit the bore of a blowgun. The fins inside the cone used to keep the ink cartridge straight will keep an inserted shaft perfectly centered. However, the hole is big and only wooden shafts such as bamboo barbeque spits will be big and light enough to make a good dart.

You can find wood beads in arts and crafts shops with center holes drilled through. They are sold in a pack of 18 pieces and cost about $1.00. They come in 8, 10, 12, and 20 mm sizes. There are also $\frac{1}{2}$-inch wood balls that can be used as stun beads.

Fortune beads that are made into bracelets are even cheaper. A 36-piece pack costs about $1.00. They have center-drilled holes bigger than the size of bamboo spits. However, with a generous amount of glue, it can be used as a tail for a bamboo spit. They are even brightly painted.

There is a good chance that you will find plastic beads on a necklace in a thrift shop. I found an 80-bead necklace that cost $1.00. To enlarge the hole, heat the shaft then insert it in the bead. (Do not use a candle because the heated part will become coated with soot.)

MAKING OR PREPARING THE SHAFT

The shaft can be wooden or metallic. Both are readily available or can be fashioned from materials that are designed for other purposes.

METALLIC SHAFTS. Piano wire with diameters of $\frac{1}{32}$-inch or $\frac{1}{16}$-inch in lengths of 36 inches can be obtained from mail order houses. The $\frac{1}{16}$-inch wire is quite heavy. The shafts of commer-

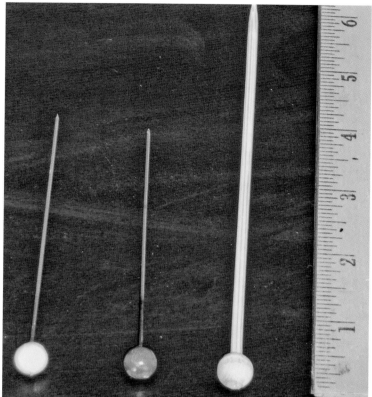

FIGURE 4-6. Bead tails (left to right): from a necklace, a commercial dart, and a wood ball. Broken rosary beads can be fitted with bamboo spits.

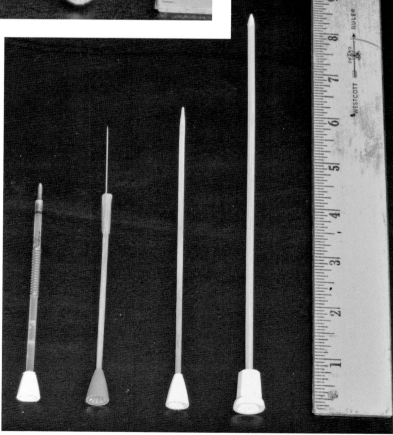

FIGURE 4-7. At extreme left is a dart made entirely from a ball pen. The middle two are darts with tail cones cut from ball pens with wooden shafts (one is tipped with a sewing needle). At extreme right is a wooden dart with a tail taken from the twine of a Venetian blind.

cial darts are $\frac{1}{32}$-inch thick. The good thing about the 36 inch long piano wire is that you can cut it to the desired length. Most commercial darts come in 3- or 4-inch lengths.

Bicycles spokes, nails, and hangers are good sources of metallic shafts. They can be cut to the desired length then inserted into a tail. Straightened paper clips and thin copper wire can be used as shafts. Do not remove the head of nails for use with homemade paper, plastic, or aluminum cone tails. The head will secure the nail against the sides of the cone and prevent it from wiggling.

WOODEN SHAFTS. You can make wooden shafts from bamboo barbeque spits. Bamboo makes an excellent shaft because it has long fibers, has great tensile strength and is easy to work with.

You can also make shafts from bamboo chopsticks but you have to whittle it down to reduce its weight and diameter.

In the Philippines there is a broom used to sweep leaves called *walis tinting*. The tinting is the spine of a palm leaf. It is thin and straight.

The tips of bamboo spits are sharp but must be fire-hardened. With repeated use, its tip will need to be sharpened then eventually discarded when it becomes too short after repeated re-sharpening.

You can split (or use a very thin saw) the bamboo spit to insert a sewing needle. Doll needles may be used also but they can cost as much as $2.00 each. Apply glue to the composite tip then bind it with adhesive tape.

THE ASSEMBLED DART

Whether the shaft is metal or wood, when inserted into a wooden or plastic tail, apply a generous amount of glue. Wipe off excess glue to minimize air resistance.

While it only takes a few minutes to make a dart, to make one that will shoot straight is another matter. For example, in a couple of minutes, you can make a dart using a plastic sheet for a cone tail. It might appear that the dart is properly made. Until you shoot it.

The weight of the cone will not be uniform because of the necessary overlap that also has to be taped. The adhesive tape can become unglued during the flight of the dart. The non-uniform weight of the cone and the ungluing of the adhesive tape can make the dart do undesired aerobatics.

TO BUY OR TO MAKE

If you enjoy working with your hands, a good project will be to make a dart from parts of a ball pen, a shaft from a barbecue spit, and a point from a sewing needle (Figure 4-10).

To make the dart shown in Figure 4-7, second from left

- Unscrew (or saw if necessary) the front cone part of the ball pen.
- Try to fit a bamboo spit in its hole. If the spit is too big, cut the nose of the cone until the bamboo spit fits in its hole.

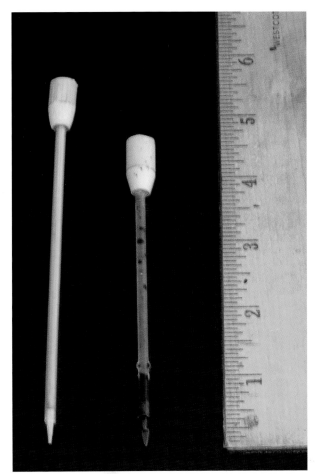

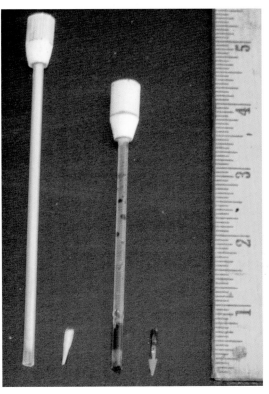

FIGURE 5-2. Detachable tip. At left is a hollow shaft from a drinking straw (the type used on juice boxes) provided with a detachable bamboo spit point. At right is a hollow shaft made from a ball pen ink cartridge provided with a detachable copper arrowhead. The tails are bullet-nosed wood dowels.

A metallic shaft can be weakened by treating it with acid, by allowing it to rust, or by notching it with a file. The weakened section will break off either at impact or when the target attempts to pull it out.

DETACHABLE TIP. Detachable points are not difficult to make. However, you will need a hollow shaft.

Empty ink cartridges of ball pens are a good source of hollow shafts. Most are plastic but occasionally you will find a metallic one.

Use up the ink, which will require a lot of writing, then remove its metallic tip by sawing it off. Plug the hollow on the shorter side of the pinch (with the proper length of a bamboo spit) to prevent the point from disappearing inside the shaft. Insert the point into the hollow and attach a tail to the cartridge. You will need to shave off material from the spit to make it fit the cartridge.

The length of the bamboo spit used as a plug should be such that only a ⅛-inch length of the detachable point can be inserted in the remaining hollow. This will ensure that the entire detachable point becomes embedded in the target. To make the detachable point more potent, shape it into an arrowhead after hammering flat. You can make an arrowhead from a flattened copper wire.

The tiny pins on brand new polo shirts make good detachable points. After removing its head, you can insert about five of the tiny pins in the hollow of the ink cartridge. Grind the pins very short using a bench grinder. (Stick the pin into a small piece of wood so that it will be easier to handle during grinding.)

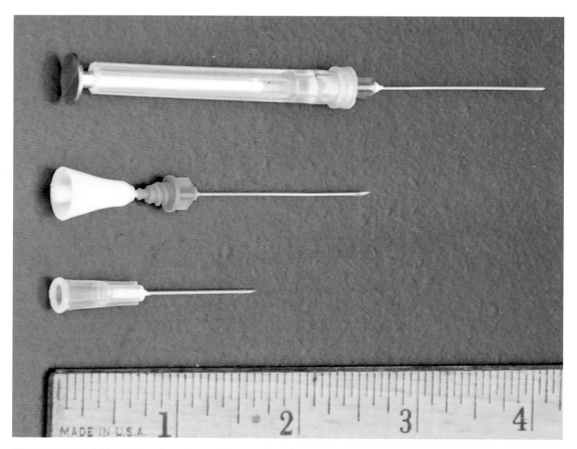

FIGURE 5-3 (A). Hypodermic needles used as darts with chemical payload (A, top to bottom): needle with a hollow vial provided with a roofing nail that serves as a plunger and tail, a 1½-inch needle inserted in a .40 caliber commercial tail cone, a needle that can be shot off very small tubes. The tails are not aerodynamically shaped and can only be shot accurately from less than 15 feet. The two needles at the top right (B) can be shot from drinking straws.

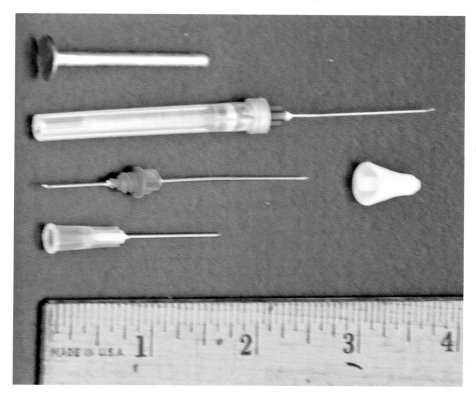

FIGURE 5-3 (B).

One other good source of a hollow shaft is the small drinking straw (typically about 5½ inches) used with juice boxes. To make the straw more rigid and heavier, insert a bamboo spit 5⅛ inches long in it. This will leave a ⅛-inch hollow for the insertion of the detachable point.

You can notch the head of commercial steel darts with a file to weaken it and make it breakable.

DARTS WITH CHEMICAL PAYLOAD

Back in the Philippines, I worked in a research and development laboratory. There was one particular day of the year that I did not like participating in: the yearly inventory of chemicals. We had to know what chemicals we risked running out of at the wrong time. Safety was not one of the priorities of the company. We were not provided with facemasks.

In the evening, I lectured at a nearby university. One of the subjects I taught was a laboratory course in physical chemistry.

All the chemicals in the two laboratories could be used as irritants or outright poisons. The only differences between the chemicals are the smell and the doses at which they become deadly. Some are potential explosives—alone or in a mix with other chemicals.

Chemicals are potentially dangerous. So are darts. A dart becomes even more dangerous when it can deliver a chemical payload from a safe distance.

The simplest way to deliver a chemical payload is by dipping the point of the dart in it. However, you have to modify its shaft. A bamboo shaft can be pitted by repeatedly stabbing with a sharp point. Dipping it for a short time in acid can pit a steel shaft. You can purposely make part of the shaft rust by coating all but its last 2" from the point with nail polish. You can then wet the uncovered portion with water and allow it to rust.

An even better way to deliver a small amount of a chemical payload is by making the shaft from a hypodermic needle. Dip the needle in the chemical. Surface tension will cause the chemical to go up the needle.

A hypodermic needle comes in a small plastic vial. In about half an hour, you can make the hypodermic needle into a dart with a hollow shaft. When you test this dart, make sure you are not shooting into wood. Even when used on cardboard targets, a hypodermic needle will bend easily.

Use a new dart if you are to deliver a chemical payload. Because the opening at the needle's tip is tiny, make sure it is not clogged. Before shooting, place the tip on tissue paper then check the paper for liquid. If liquid passed to it then the needle is not clogged and will deliver the payload as designed.

OTHER DARTS

You can remove the contents of a desiccant and replace it with a liquid or powder or even with a message.

You can replace the cap with a thin sheet of paper that would break at impact. This will spill its contents at the target.

chapter 6

CONCEPTUAL
PHYSICS
OF THE BLOWGUN

A dart in flight will follow a parabolic path called its trajectory, ideally. However, air resistance will shorten its parabolic path. Neglecting air resistance, the motion of a dart in flight can be described by the formula

$$y = x \tan \alpha - \frac{g}{2v_0^2 \cos^2 \alpha} x^2 \qquad (6\text{-}1)$$

We will examine the quantities y, x, g, α and v_0.

VARIABLES IN THE FLIGHT OF A DART

VERTICAL DISTANCE, Y - This is the vertical distance between the centers of gravity (CG) of the dart as it emerges from the barrel of the blowgun and as it sticks on the target. For example, if the dart is launched 5 feet off the ground and sticks on the target 5 feet off the ground, y = 5 - 5 = 0. If the dart is launched 5 feet off the ground and sticks on the target 5 feet 6 inches off the ground y = 5 feet 6 inches - 5 feet = 6 inches (or 0.5 inches).

INITIAL VELOCITY, v_0 - This is the velocity of the dart as it emerges from the barrel. Equation (6-1) does not apply to the dart when it is still in the barrel since it will be sliding against the wall although we will assume that the barrel is frictionless.

ANGLE OF LAUNCH, α - This is the angle that the CG of the dart makes with the horizontal as it emerges from the barrel. This is the angle at which you will aim your blowgun.

HORIZONTAL DISTANCE, x - This is the distance traveled by the dart (by its CG) in its trajectory until it hits the target. As soon as the dart makes contact with the target, Equation (6-1) no longer applies.

ACCELERATION DUE TO GRAVITY, G - This is the force exerted by gravity on the dart and has the value 32.2 ft/sec^2 (9.8 m/s^2). Gravity causes the path of the dart to become curved.

The first question that comes to mind is "What is the velocity of the dart as it emerges from the barrel?"

You can measure the velocity of the dart if you have access to high speed measuring instruments. I constructed and used a ballistic pendulum to measure the speed of darts I shoot from my blowgun. See Section 18, Appendix A.

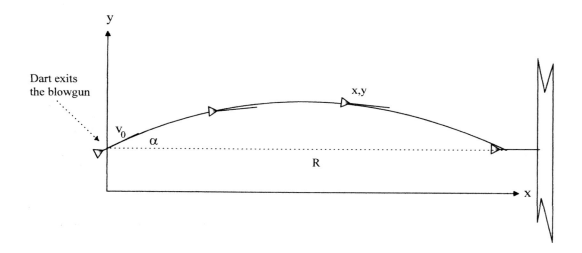

FIGURE 6-1. The trajectory of a dart shot from a blowgun will follow a parabolic curve. It is the center of gravity of the dart that will trace a parabolic curve. (Unless otherwise specified, this and other sketches are not drawn to scale.)

VELOCITY OF THE DART

The closest thing to blowing air into the barrel of a blowgun is a cough. The air expelled during a cough can have velocities between 75 mph (100 ft/sec or 33.5 m/sec) and 100 mph (146.7 ft/sec or 44.7 m/sec). It is reasonable to assume that a person can blow air into the mouthpiece of a blowgun at the speed of a cough. With this in mind, we will check out the velocity with which blowgun hunters in Ecuador shoot their darts.

Author John Man[3] lived among the Waoranis of Ecuador and gave a first hand account of their skill in the use of the blowgun. He wrote, "... an experienced hunter could shoot a dart 360 feet or more horizontally and up to 200 feet vertically." John Man himself was able to shoot a dart 300 feet horizontally using a 9½-foot blowgun. We will determine the velocities of the horizontal (Figure 6-2) and vertical (Figure 6-3) shots.

We will consider 360 feet as the Waorani's maximum range. The maximum range of a projectile is

$$R = (v_0^2 \sin 2\alpha)/g$$

For maximum range α must be 450. With R = 360 ft and g = 32.2 ft/sec², v_0 computes to the value 107.7 ft/sec. This velocity is well under 146.7 ft/sec, the maximum velocity of a cough.

The maximum height that can be attained by a projectile is

$$H = (v_0^2 \sin^2 \alpha)/2g$$

(6-2)

H will be maximum if $\sin^2\alpha$ is equal to 1, that is when α is 90 degrees. Hence, the blowgun must be aimed directly overhead. With H = 200 ft and g = 32.2 ft/sec², v_0 computes to the value 113 ft/sec. Again, this velocity is well under the maximum velocity of a cough. The velocities with which the dart is expelled from the blowgun for the horizontal and vertical shots are within an order of magnitude (107.7 ft/sec versus 113 ft/sec) of each other.

A dart velocity of 107.7 ft/sec will seem to be too slow for the Waoranis who obviously have very strong lungs. However, friction between the tail and the barrel will reduce the velocity of the dart. In flight, the non-streamlined flow of air over the outer surface of the kapok tail as well as through the spaces between kapok fibers and high humidity will further slow down the dart. One also has to note that the Waorani blowgun has an inside bore of at least ½-inch.

Even the Waorani will have difficulty holding a 10-foot blowgun that weighs at least 10 lbs steady while aiming at a target at or nearly horizontal. Of course, he can rest the blowgun on a tree branch. But his targets are mostly in the treetops: the woolly monkey and the nocturnal pheasant-sized curassow. For this reason, the Waorani would get under his target and aim his blowgun overhead at a steep angle.

Legend[4] has it that the Jivaros are so skilled with their blowguns that they can hit a hummingbird from 50 yards. Since they also live and hunt in the Ecuadorian forests, we can assume that they can shoot as well as the Waoranis and that the Jivaro dart will exit the blowgun at 110 ft/sec.

The blowgun can be aimed at different elevations where the dart would be launched at different angles (Figure 6-4). However, it is best to aim the blowgun at the smallest possible angle from the horizontal to shoot accurately.

For the Jivaro to be able to achieve such a feat, he must have (a) excellent eyesight so he can pick out the hummingbird from the background foliage (b) great lung power (c) a straight blowgun, and (d) lots of practice. Obviously, the Jivaro possesses all these.

We will assume that the dart exits the blowgun 5' off the ground and hits the hummingbird also 5' off the ground.

For this special case where y = 0, the range R, of the dart is given by the formula

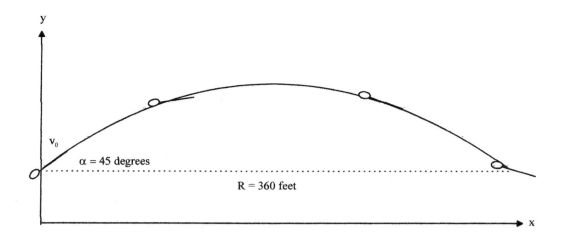

FIGURE 6-2. The maximum horizontal range for the Waorani's dart is 360 feet. The dimension of the dart is highly exaggerated.

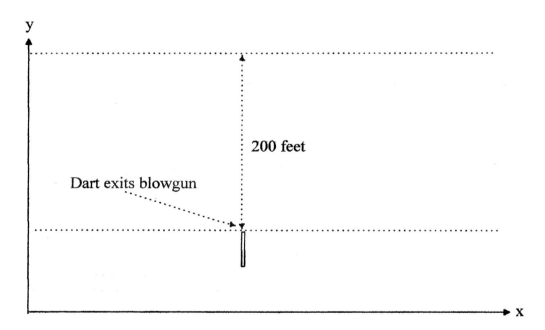

FIGURE 6-3. The maximum vertical height of the Waorani's dart. The Waorani is able to bring down woolly monkeys from 100 feet up. With an initial velocity of 113 ft/sec, it will take the dart about 1.0 sec to reach the monkey and to impact with a velocity of 47 ft/sec.

$$R = \frac{v_0^2 \sin 2\alpha}{g} \tag{6-3}$$

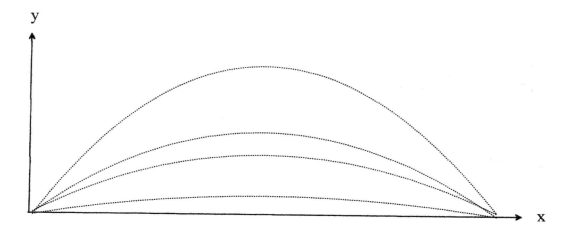

FIGURE 6-4. Four of the many possible trajectories of a dart shot from a blowgun. A more accurate way of shooting is to aim the blowgun at a small angle. (See Figure 9-11.)

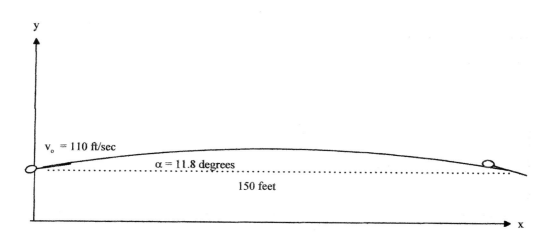

FIGURE 6-5. The trajectory of a Jivaro dart shot at a hummingbird from 50 yards.

It will be easier to hit the hummingbird if the blowgun is aimed as close to horizontal as possible. Hence, with the range $R = 150$ ft, $g = 32.2$ ft/sec^2 and $v_0 = 110$ ft/sec, we can solve for the likely angle that the Jivaro will launch his dart. We find that the Jivaro has to aim his blowgun at 11.8° from the horizontal. However, he has to aim higher because air resistance will reduce the velocity of the dart.

That the Jivaro can hit a small target from 50 yards cannot be doubted. However, who would want to shoot at such a small target? Most hummingbirds[5] are about 2 inches measured from bill to tail and weigh about 0.07 oz. See Figure 13-2.

Contained in each blowgun package marketed by United Cutlery are recommended shooting ranges as well as the effective ranges of blowguns of different lengths (Table 6-1).

TABLE 6-1

Length of blowgun, inches	Gun shooting range, feet
18	30
24	40
30	50
36	70
42	90
48	110
54	125
The effective range is $\frac{1}{3}$ to $\frac{1}{2}$ of the shooting range.	

I use a 1-foot 7-inch blowgun for shooting at a target from 10 to 15 feet, a 2-foot 4-inch blowgun from 20 to 30 feet; a 3-foot 5-inch blowgun from 30 to 40 feet; a two-piece 4-inch 5-inch blowgun from 30 to 50 feet and a 5-foot blowgun from 50 feet to 60 feet. Why?

Consider the mea hua needle. When you blow through the goose feather, a column of air will push the dart 2 inches until it emerges from the tube.

During the time of contact, the air you blow produces a change in the velocity of the dart. Using Newton's second law of motion, we can obtain a relationship between the average force (F) of the blow, the time (t) of interaction and change in velocity. A very useful quantity obtained from this relationship is called impulse.

Impulse is defined as

$$I = Ft = mv_f - mv_i \tag{6-4}$$

where m is the mass of the dart. Impulse is the product of the average force exerted and the time the force remains in contact with the tail cone. The initial and final velocities of the dart are v_i and v_f respectively. Since the dart is initially at rest, $v_i = 0$ and equation (6-4) simplifies to

$$I = Ft = mv_f \tag{6-5}$$

We can get some idea on the effect of the length of the blowgun on the velocity of the dart in the barrel. Consider a 3-foot and a 5-foot blowgun. The distance (length of the barrel d) traveled by the dart inside the barrel is

$$d = v_f t \quad \text{or} \quad t = \frac{d}{v_f} \tag{6-6}$$

Substituting this value of t into equation (6-5) yields

$$F\frac{d}{v_f} = mv_f \quad \text{or} \quad Fd = mv_f^2 \tag{6-7}$$

Solving for the velocity of the dart in the 5-foot long blowgun we get

$$v_{f5} = \sqrt{5\frac{F}{m}} \tag{6-8}$$

For the 3-foot long blowgun

$$v_{f3} = \sqrt{3\frac{F}{m}} \tag{6-9}$$

We find that the ratio of the velocities of the dart in the 5-foot long blowgun to that of the dart in the 3-foot long blowgun is

$$v_{f5} = 1.3v_{f3} \tag{6-10}$$

The shooter, after years of practice, will inhale approximately the same quantity of air and will blow through the tube approximately with the same average force. In my case, the force of my blow would be approximately the same whether I am shooting a 3-foot or a 5-foot long blowgun. The consistency of the force of my blow is a result of the more than 500,000 times I have shot .40 caliber darts. Since for this analysis I used the same dart, the quantity F/m cancelled out when (6-8) was divided by (6-9).

Equation (6-10) shows that the exit velocity of the dart from the 5-foot long blowgun will be 1.3 times that of the dart from the 3-foot blowgun. This ratio could change for the occasional shooter because the average force with which he shoots could vary greatly. However, it will not change the mathematical conclusion and real life experience that *a dart shot from a longer blowgun will have a longer range than a dart shot from a shorter blowgun.*

A longer blowgun will be more accurate. This, we will establish.

We can re-write (6-5) as

$$v_f = \frac{F}{m}t \tag{6-11}$$

The mass of the dart is a constant. If t is greater, vf will have a greater value. This is accomplished by shooting a longer blowgun where the dart will stay in the barrel much longer.

For example: In the longer 3-foot 5-inch blowgun, a column of air will exert a force on the tail cone until it has traveled the whole length of the barrel. The 3-foot 5-inch blowgun is more than 20 times longer than the 2-inch mea hua needle. Thus, the .40 caliber dart will be inside the barrel longer, will be pushed by a longer column of air and will exit the blowgun at a much greater velocity. With a greater velocity, the angle of launch will be smaller.

This is stated in (6-2). We will re-write it as

$$\sin \alpha = \frac{Rg}{v_f^2} \tag{6-12}$$

Equation (6-12) shows that as v_f increases, sin 2a decreases (the value of the right side of the equation becomes less). Hence, the blowgun can be aimed at a flatter trajectory. A table of values of v_0 and angle of launch are shown in Table 6-2. Here, the target is 33 feet away. The dart is launched 5 feet off the ground and hits the target 5 feet off the ground.

Table 6-2 shows that you can aim the tip of your blowgun at the target at a very small angle from the horizontal if the velocity of the dart is great enough. Here, with an initial velocity of 146 ft/sec, the angle of launch is 0.5 degrees. At 60 ft/sec, the angle of launch is 2.6 degrees. (See the aiming configuration illustrated in Figure 9-11.)

TABLE 6-2. Shooting distance is 33 feet

Initial velocity, v_0 ft/sec	Angle of launch, degrees
60	2.6
70	1.9
80	1.5
90	1.2
100	1.0
146	0.5

DIAMETER OF THE BORE

I used the .40 caliber blowgun for my first 500,000 shots. After my book *Pananandata Guide to Sport Blowguns* was published in 1999, I felt drained mentally and did not shoot my blowgun again until about 4 years later. When I resumed shooting, I decided to shoot the .625 caliber blowgun.

My very first shot missed badly. For this reason, I decided to analyze the relationships between volumetric flow rate and the velocity of the air blown through the .40 caliber and the .625 Magnum blowguns. We will examine four cases where

- $V_4 = V_6$ – We will blow V_4 through the .40 and .625 caliber blowguns and determine the relationship between v_6 and v_4. V_4 is the volumetric flow rate through the .40 caliber blowgun.

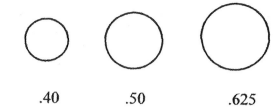

.40 .50 .625

FIGURE 6-6. Actual sizes of the blowguns I used to generate the learning curves illustrated in Section 12.

- $v_6 = v_4$ – We will determine the relationship between V_4 and V_6. v_4 is the velocity of the air that pushes the .40 caliber dart.
- $v_6 = 1.2v_4$ – We will determine the relationship between V_4 and V_6. It is claimed that the velocity attained by a .625 caliber dart is 20% faster than a dart shot from a .40 caliber blowgun.
- $V_6 = V_4$ - We will blow V_6 through the .40 and .625 caliber blowguns and determine the relationship between v_6 and v_4.

We do not need to know the actual values of the volume of the air inhaled and the velocity with which it is expelled from the lungs. We can use dimensional analysis to come to some logical conclusions.

We have first to establish several definitions.

- A .40 caliber blowgun has a ³⁄₈-inch bore or a radius of ³⁄₁₆-inch; a .625 caliber blowgun, a ⁵⁄₈-inch bore or a radius of ⁵⁄₁₆-inch.

- Velocity v = ft/sec
    v_4 = velocity of the air blown through the .40 caliber dart
    v_6 = velocity of the air blown through the .625 caliber dart

- Volumetric flow, $V = ft^3/sec$
    V_4 = flow through .40 caliber blowgun
    V_6 = flow through .625 caliber blowgun

- Cross sectional area, $A = ft^2$
    $A_4 = 3.14(^3/_{16})^2$, area of .40 caliber blowgun
    $A_6 = 3.14(^5/_{16})^2$, area of .625 caliber blowgun
    D_4 = diameter of .40 caliber blowgun
    D_6 = diameter of .625 caliber blowgun
    $A_4/A_6 = (^3/_5)^2$
    $A_6/A_4 = (^5/_3)^2$

- Mass
    m_4 = mass of the .40 caliber dart
    m_6 = mass of the .625 caliber dart

CASE 1. Volumetric flow rate of air (V_4) in the .40 caliber blowgun is used to propel the dart in the .625 caliber blowgun.

The velocities with which the air will be expelled through the blowguns are $v_4 = V_4/A_4$ and $v_6 = V_6/A_6$.

With long years of practice, the blowgun shooter would inhale, consistently, approximately the same amount of air to fill his lungs. Thus, if he had practiced solely with the .40 caliber blowgun, approximately the same flow rate will be expelled from his lungs. If he does, we can compute the resulting velocity of the air blown through the .625 caliber blowgun.

$$V_4 = V_6 \quad \text{and} \quad v_6 A_6 = v_4 A_4 \quad \text{or}$$
(6-13)

$$v_6 = v_4(A_4/A_6) = (3/5)^2 v_4 \quad \text{or}$$
(6-13a)

$$v_6 = 0.36 v_4$$
(6-14)

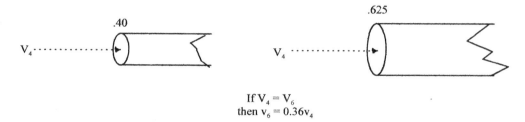

If $V_4 = V_6$
then $v_6 = 0.36 v_4$

FIGURE 6-7. Case I.

Thus, with the same volume of air expelled from the shooter's lungs, the air blown through the .625 caliber blowgun will have a velocity that is approximately ⅓ less than that of the air blown through a .40 caliber blowgun. This is why my first shot using the .625 caliber blowgun hit about 3 feet below my target.

We will assume that the ratio $v_6/v_4 = 0.36$ is the same ratio of the exit velocities of the darts in the two blowguns. With this assumption, we will compare the maximum range of each blowgun. The maximum range in shooting the .40 caliber blowgun is $R_4 = v_4^2/g$ (Equation 6-2).

If I shoot the .625 blowgun using the normal volume of air I use on the .40 caliber blowgun, the maximum range, R_6, I could reach would be $R_6 = (0.36 v_4)^2/g$. Combining the equations for R_4 and R_6, there results $R_6 = 0.13 R_4$. If my maximum range for shooting the .40 caliber blowgun is 300 feet, my dart could travel only 39 feet if I shoot the .625 caliber blowgun using the same volumetric flow rate I used in the smaller .40 caliber blowgun. This is illustrated in Figure 6-8.

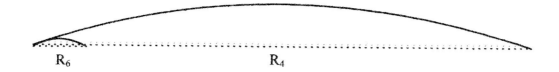

R_6 R_4

FIGURE 6-8. The maximum ranges for the .625 and .40 caliber blowguns when the volumetric flow rate used to propel the darts is V_4. It is assumed that the two darts are of equal weight.

CASE 2. Volumetric flow rate of the air required if the dart is to be propelled in the two blowguns with the same velocity, v_4.

We will assume, with practice, that we can propel a dart inside the two blowguns at the same velocity. Thus,

$$v_6 = v_4 \tag{6-15}$$

$$v_4 = V_4 / A_4 \tag{6-16}$$

$$v_6 = V_6 / A_6 \tag{6-17}$$

$$V_4 / A_4 = V_6 / A_6 \tag{6-18}$$

$$V_6 = V_4 (A_6 / A_4) = (5/3)^2 V_4 \tag{6-18a}$$

$$V_6 = 2.8 V_4 \tag{6-19}$$

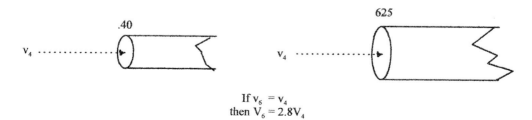

If $v_6 = v_4$
then $V_6 = 2.8 V_4$

FIGURE 6-9. Case 2.

Thus, if the dart were to be propelled with the same velocity, the air flow rate through the .625 blowgun has to be about 3 times that through the .40 caliber blowgun.

It will require a great deal of re-training (shooting the blowgun) to inhale then expel this much air through your trachea (windpipe).

CASE 3. It is claimed that the velocity of the dart shot through the .625 blowgun is 20% greater than that of the .40 caliber blowgun, that is, $v_6 = 1.2v_4$. This figure, 20%, must have been determined experimentally.

$$v_6 = 1.2v_4 \quad \text{or} \tag{6-20}$$

$$V_6/A_6 = 1.2(V_4/A_4) \quad \text{or} \tag{6-21}$$

$$V_6 = 3.33V_4 \tag{6-22}$$

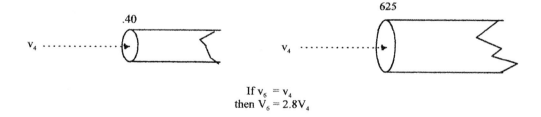

If $v_6 = v_4$
then $V_6 = 2.8V_4$

FIGURE 6-10. Case 3.

Thus, the shooter will have to blow air through the .625 blowgun at a rate that is more than 3 times that through a .40 caliber blowgun. This is tantamount to all of a sudden acquiring another pair of lungs. But, all healthy shooters are stuck with one pair of lungs that has a maximum holding capacity. Just because the shooter uses a .625 caliber blowgun does not automatically give him a stronger pair of lungs.

Hence, if you are used to shooting the .40 caliber blowgun, you will find that blowing through a .625 blowgun is a much more difficult.

CASE 4. Volumetric flow rate of air (V6) in the .625 caliber blowgun is used to propel the dart in the .40 caliber blowgun.

We will propel the .40 caliber dart through the .40 caliber blowgun using the volumetric flow rate for the .625 caliber blowgun.

$$v_4 = V_4/A_4 \tag{6-23}$$

$$v_6 = V_6/A_6 \tag{6-24}$$

Since $V_6 = V_4$, combining equation (6-23) and (6-24) yields

$$v_4 = (A_6/A_4)v_6 \quad \text{or} \tag{6-25}$$

$$v_4 = 2.78v_6 \tag{6-26}$$

$$R_6 = v_6^2/g \tag{6-27}$$

$$R_4 = v_4^2/g \tag{6-28}$$

Dividing equation (6-21) by equation (6-20) results in

$$R_4 = (v_4^2/v_6^2)R_6 \tag{6-29}$$

Substitute v_4 from equation (6-26) into equation (6-29) yields

$$R_4 = 7.73R_6 \tag{6-30}$$

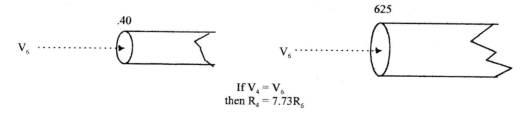

If $V_4 = V_6$
then $R_4 = 7.73R_6$

FIGURE 6-11. Case 4.

Thus, the .40 caliber dart will have roughly 8 times the range when the much larger V6 flow rate is used to blow through the .40 caliber blow gun.

MASS OF THE DART

The mass (m) of the dart will not influence its trajectory as indicated by its absence from equation (6-1). However, inside the barrel, the mass of the dart matters. We will examine the effect of a heavier dart on its velocity inside the barrel. (This should be differentiated from the velocity of the dart in flight.)

A .625 caliber dart is 3 times heavier than the .40 caliber dart. Thus

$$m_6 = 3m_4 \qquad (6\text{-}31)$$

It is claimed that the dart is 20% faster.

$$v_6 = 1.2v_4 \qquad (6\text{-}32)$$

Recall that

$$I = Ft = mv_f$$

The impulse for the .625 caliber blowgun is

$$F_6 t_6 = m_6 v_6 \qquad (6\text{-}33)$$

The impulse for the .40 caliber blowgun is

$$F_4 t_4 = m_4 v_4 \qquad (6\text{-}34)$$

We can combine the two equations to get

$$F_6 t_6 / F_4 t_4 = m_6 v_6 / m_4 v_4 \qquad (6\text{-}34a)$$

Substituting the values of $m_6 = 3m_4$ and $v_6 = 1.2\, v_4$ yields

$$F_6 t_6 = 3.6 F_4 t_4 \qquad (6\text{-}35)$$

The impulse required to propel the .625 caliber dart is 3.6 times that required to propel the .40 caliber dart. This will put great burden on the lungs. Hence, before you shoot this blowgun, you should consult your physician.

FORCE OF IMPACT

It is possible to determine the force of impact F of the dart on the target. Figure 6-12 shows the variables involved in the launching of the dart.

The measurable quantities are:

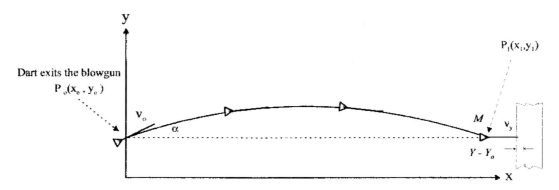

FIGURE 6-12. The dart travels on a parabolic curve

- v_o the initial velocity of the dart can be measured with a chronograph
- α the angle at which the dart is launched can be measured with a compass
- M the dart can be weighed to get its mass
- $Y - Y_o$ the depth of penetration of the dart can be measured with a ruler
- v_y the impact velocity of the dart can be measured with a second chronograph. If we have only one chronograph, we have to find this value in some other way or we can measure v_o then move the chronograph to the target to measure v_y. In this exercise, the chronograph is placed near the target to measure v_y.

The force of impact F of the dart can be found using Newton's Second Law of Motion. It is given by

$$F = M(a_y + g)$$

(6-36)

where M is the mass of the dart, ay is the acceleration (deceleration of the dart) and g is 9.8 m/s². We have one equation but we have two unknowns: F and ay. We need to find a_y.

The dart shot from a distance will become embedded in the target as shown in Figure 6-13. The equation that applies to the deceleration of the dart is

$$Y - Y_o = \frac{(v^2 - v_y^2)}{2a_y}$$

(6-37)

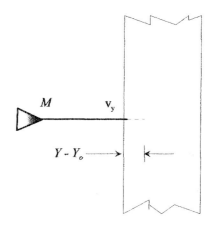

FIGURE 6-13. The dart becomes embedded 1 cm deep on the target after being shot from a blowgun. After its energy is spent, it comes to a stop.

where v is the final velocity of the dart.

Consider a dart with a mass of 8.5 x 10⁻⁴ kg that penetrated 1 cm deep into the target. Since the dart will come to a stop, the final velocity. The velocity at the point of impact was measured to be 30 m/s. Substitute the given values in (6-37).

$$0.01 = \frac{(0 - 30^2)}{2a_y}$$

$$a_y = -45000 \quad \text{m/s} \qquad (6\text{-}38)$$

$$F = 8 * 10^{-4}(-45000 + 9.8)$$

$$F = -36.8 \quad \text{newtons}$$

Note that the minus (-) sign indicates the direction of F.

It requires 3,111 newtons[6] to break a 1 x 20 x 30 cm pine board that is normally used in karate demonstrations.

The kinetic energy of the dart at the point of impact is

$$E_k = \frac{1}{2}Mv_y^2 \qquad (6\text{-}39)$$

Substitute the known values

$$E_k = \frac{1}{2}(8 * 10^{-4})(30^2) = 0.4 \quad \text{joules}$$

It requires about 18 joules[7] to break the arm bone.

chapter 7

BREATHING

Do breathing exercises before you shoot. Breathing exercises are designed to give you a good feeling, to fill you with energy, and to put you in the proper frame of mind for the shoot.

YIN BREATHING[8]

Place both hands in front of your face. Make your index finger tips touch and place your thumbs on each side of your nose (Figure 7-1).

- Press your left thumb against your left nostril to close it. Breathe in through your right nostril slowly until you cannot take in any more air. Exhale through the right nostril just as slowly until all it feels like there is no more air in your lungs.

- Remove your left thumb from your left nostril and press your right thumb on your right nostril to close it. Breathe in through the left nostril slowly

FIGURE 7-1. Yin breathing exercise.

until you have filled your lungs. Exhale through the left nostril slowly until it feels like there is no more air in your lungs.

Ensure that the closure of one nostril is simultaneous with the freeing of the other and that your breathing (breathe in and exhale) is continuous.

If you feel obstructions in your breathing, consult your doctor to determine if it is safe for you to shoot.

YANG BREATHING

- Let your hands hang by your side (Figure 7-2A).

FIGURE 7-2B TO FIGURE 7-2C
- Breathe in through your nose slowly and raise your hands in front of your chest (Figure 7-2B).

- Exhale slowly and forcefully (with a smooth hissing sound) through your mouth as you push slowly and forcefully forward with your open palms (Figure 7-2C). Your elbow should be just short of being fully extended at the end of your exhale.

FIGURE 7-2B TO FIGURE 7-2D
- Breathe in slowly through your nose as you pull back your hands in front of your chest (Figure 7-2B).

- Exhale slowly and forcefully (with a smooth hissing sound) through your mouth as you push slowly and forcefully to your side with your open palms (Figure 7-2D). Your elbow should be just short of being fully extended at the end of your exhale.

FIGURE 7-2B TO FIGURE 7-2E
- Breathe in slowly through your nose as you pull back your hands in front of your chest (Figure 7-2B).

- Exhale slowly and forcefully (with a smooth hissing sound) through your mouth as you push slowly and forcefully upward (Figure 7-2E) with your open palms. Your elbow should be just short of being fully extended at the end of your exhale.

FIGURE 7-2B TO FIGURE 7-2F
- Breathe in slowly through your nose as you pull back your hands in front of your chest (Figure 7-2B).

- Exhale slowly and forcefully (with a smooth hissing sound) through your mouth as you push slowly and forcefully downward with your open palms (Figure 7-2F). Your elbow should be just short of being fully extended at the end of your exhale.

FIGURE 7-2.
The yang
breathing exercise.

A

B

C

D

E

F

If you have never shot a blowgun before, you might experience some soreness in your throat in the beginning. If you do, it will be wise to wait a day or two before you resume shooting.

BLOWING AIR THROUGH THE BARREL

The explosive propulsion of air from the lungs occurs when a person coughs at which time the trachea (windpipe) contracts. A bad cough will hurt. Hence, we would not want to blow air through a blowgun at a speed that could result in a sore throat. With practice and with experience, we will be able to propel a dart, consistently, at a velocity that would not result in any discomfort.

I have not felt any discomfort when shooting a .40 caliber or a .50 caliber blowgun. However, shooting the .625 caliber blowgun with its 3-gram dart will become like having a bad cough after a while. Indeed, after shooting the .625 caliber blowgun 6,000 times in 60 days, I felt soreness in my right ribs and in my back at the right side. I had to stop shooting for a while. When I resumed shooting the .625 caliber blowgun, I shot only 25 darts a day. There was no recurrence of the pain.

When the shooter shoots the blowgun, his windpipe (trachea) contracts from its normal radius r_n to the radius r during the blow (Figure 7-3).

The mathematical equation[10] correlating the velocity of the expelled air and the radius of the trachea before and during a cough is shown in (7-1). Since the sudden expulsion of air through the trachea is but a "controlled cough," we can apply this equation to the shooting of a blowgun. The equation is

$$v = k(r_n - r)r^2$$

(7-1)

where k is a constant. To find the radius at which the velocity v is maximized, differentiate (7-1) to compute for the first then the second derivative of v with respect to r. We find that the air velocity is maximized when $r = 2r_n / 3$. Thus, the maximum velocity of the air expelled occurs when the trachea contracts from its original diameter of 0.62 - 0.70 inch to 0.41 - 0.47 inch. This just happens to be very close to the inside diameter of the .40 caliber blowgun which is 0.375 inch. This will explain why most shooters use the .40 caliber blowgun.

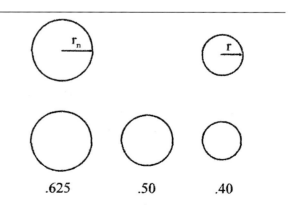

FIGURE 7-3. The trachea[9] connects the mouth and the nose to the lungs and is between 3.9 to 4.7 inches (10-12 cm) in length and has a diameter between 0.62 to 0.7 inch (16-18 mm). This diagram illustrates the relative sizes of the trachea (normal and contracted) and the bores of commercial blowguns.

chapter 8

TARGETS

Several considerations have to be taken into account when you set up your target. These include: the target, the size of the backdrop, and the location of your shoot.
You can set up your target indoors or outdoors. However, whether you set it up in one or the other location, the most important consideration is safety.

THE TARGET AND BACKDROP

Use a target that consists of a set of concentric circles with diameters of 2, 4, 6, and 8 inches (Figure 8-1) printed on an $8\frac{1}{2}$ by 11 white paper. Paste this, using carpenter's glue, on cardboard boxes that are several layers deep. You can often get the boxes, at no cost, from supermarkets. They are usually only too willing to give them to you.

You will be surprised at how deep sharp darts can become embedded in your targets. For this reason, do not use wood as targets. Otherwise, you will need a pair of pliers to pull out the darts.

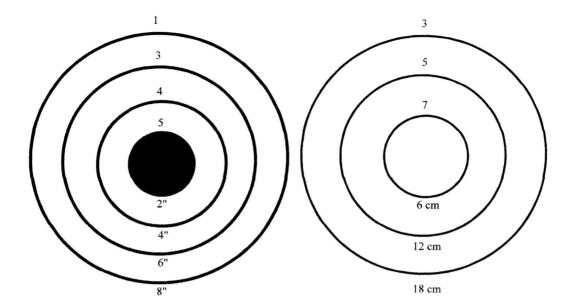

FIGURE 8-1. The target I use in my backyard consists of 4 concentric circles; that used by the International Fukiyado Association (IFA) and the Japan Sports Fukiya Association (JSFA) consists of 3 circles. The points assigned to each circle are shown at the top.

LOCATION OF YOUR SHOOT

SHOOTING INDOORS. Shooting indoors is accompanied by risks. If you live in an apartment alone, there will be no problem. You can set up your target on a diagonal across your room to have more distance to shoot from.

However, it is still possible to shoot in an apartment safely even if you live with your family. **Use ball-tipped stun darts.** For added safety, make all family members sit by your side when you shoot. You can shoot at soft targets such as pillows to avoid dart rebound. If you have a two-piece blowgun, use only one of its sections.

If you own a house with a basement, then you can shoot in relative safety.

You can prop up several layers of cardboard against a basement wall. The cardboard should be wide enough to ensure that your darts do not hit the wall. Place your target at the center of the cardboard. Should you want a higher target, you may put your cardboard target on a chair. Six layers of cardboard boxes are adequate for the 4 $^5/_{16}$-inch 0.03 oz. sharp-tipped darts. If you want to play it safe, use 8 layers. Use binder clips to clamp the cardboards together.

SHOOTING OUTDOORS. If you have a backyard of the type New York City residents have, you will have neighbors to the left, to the right and to your back—like what I once had. Shooting in such a backyard is like shooting indoors—very dangerous. Your neighbors might even call 911.

Should a big backyard be available to you, you can shoot your darts with no fear of hitting your neighbors. Still, you need to set up your target in the proper place.

SETTING UP THE TARGET

Build the target at the center of your backyard. Locate it so that the sun will be at your back all the time. If you have trees in your backyard, you should take advantage of the shade they provide during the hot days of summer. Of course, during the cold months you would want to shoot in the sun.

Landscape timber comes in 8-foot lengths. Use 4-foot sections of landscape timber to form the posts. Bury each 4-foot long timber 1½ feet deep (Figure 8-2). Space the timbers, center to center, 2 feet apart. Nail a ¾" x 2" x 4' wood on opposite sides of the landscape timber with a one-foot overlap. This will give your target a total height of 5½ feet. Place a panel of 4 feet wide, 3 feet high plywood between the tines. Clamp several layers of cardboard on the plywood backing using carpenter's clamps.

FIGURE 8-2. Target support: two pieces of wood are nailed on opposite sides of landscape timber. Viewed from the side, each one will look like a tuning fork. Place a panel of plywood between the tines then clip at least 6 layers of cardboard to it. If you are less than 6 feet tall, the top of the target support should be at the most feet 5 inches high. Otherwise, when you change the targets, you will need to tiptoe.

If you have this kind of set up, you can paste three or more targets on the cardboard (Figure 8-3B) at the desired height. I paste mine with the bull's-eye at 5' 6" or at 5' 2". Place your targets closer to the center. If the target you are aiming at is too close to the edge of the cardboard backdrop, you could lose darts during a windy-day shoot.

The reader might wonder why I didn't simply use an easel-like stand to mount my cardboard targets rather than build a seemingly unnecessarily strong target support for shooting darts that at the most weigh 3 grams. I have a good reason: I also use this set up for my knife throws.

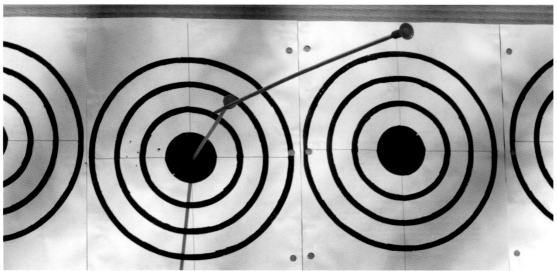

FIGURE 8-3. If you shoot more than one dart at a target, you are liable to damage already-embedded darts.

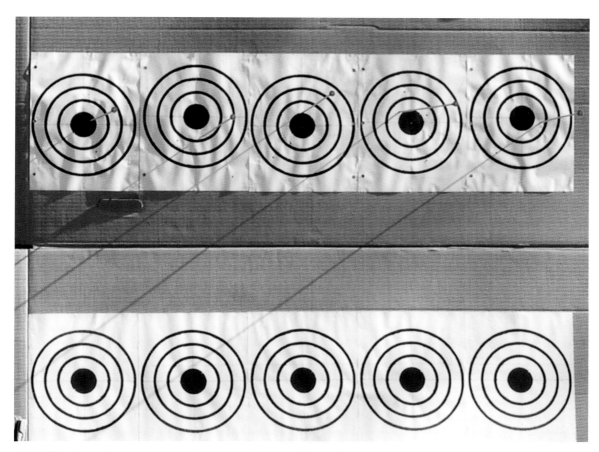

FIGURE 8-4. Shoot only one dart at each target. This will avoid damage to your darts. This set up is necessary particularly when you shoot the .625 caliber darts. After shooting, cover the target with plastic to protect it from rain. You can use old shower curtains to cover the target.

chapter 9

SHOOTING
THE BLOWGUN

Before shooting your new blowgun, always make sure that the barrel is clear. Never look up into the barrel of a blowgun as anything inside of it could fall back into your eye. To check if the barrel is clear, blow air through it. If air flows through unimpeded, you can load your dart. To double check, load your blowgun with a tail cone dart and allow it to fall through.

Avoid shooting the blowgun if there is a high pollen count.

WHAT LENGTH BLOWGUN TO USE

If you have only one blowgun, you have only one option. If you have several, the blowgun you will use will depend on the free safe space available for your shoot. I use different length blowguns for different distances as listed in Table 9-1.

TABLE 9-1

Length of blowgun	Shooting distance, feet
1 foot 7 inches	10 to 15
2 feet 4 inches	20 to 30
3 feet 5 inches	30 to 40
4 feet 5 inches (two-piece)	30 to 50
5 feet (two-piece)	30 to 50
5 feet 2 inches	60

Try shooting at a target 30 feet away using the 1-foot 7-inch blowgun. Your dart will hardly reach the target. Aim a 3-foot 5-inch blowgun at the same target. Using the 3-foot 5-inch blowgun, the dart not only will arrive at the target but also will stick with authority.

YOUR DISTANCE FROM THE TARGET

Mark your distance from the target. If you shoot on concrete, use crayons or electrical/duct tape.

In your backyard, drive wooden pegs (the ones used on corn cobs) through red ribbons (the type used on Christmas gifts) on the ground at distances of 20, 33 (10 meters), 40, and 50 feet from your target. With these markers you can shoot the same blowgun from different distances. For example, you can shoot one dart from 20 feet, a second dart from 33 feet', a third dart from 40 feet and a fourth dart from 50 feet. Of course, you also have the option to shoot all your darts from one particular distance.

PREPARING TO SHOOT

Most modern blowguns have quivers attached to the barrel. However, the quiver can only hold 10 darts and might disturb your vision. The needle-like tips of the darts are exposed when inserted in the quiver.

Place your darts in a drinking cup (Figure 9-1). Cut a paper cup and insert into the ceramic cup to make it shallower so it will be it easier to get the darts for loading into the blowgun.

Aim at 5 sets of concentric circles (Figure 8-4) to minimize the possibility of damaging the darts. If you shoot the .625 caliber blowgun, shoot only one dart at one target because if you hit an already-embedded dart, it will become unusable.

FIGURE 9-1. Darts in a drinking cup.

MECHANICS OF SHOOT-ING THE BLOWGUN

The shooting of the blowgun does not merely consist of putting a dart in the barrel then blowing air into it. If you are to derive maximum enjoyment from shooting the blowgun for sport, you have to hit your target consistently with a high degree of accuracy. In this regard, you have to master the mechanics of movements starting from the posture, the stance, to until the dart hits the target.

Before shooting the blowgun, do five repetitions of the breathing exercises shown in an earlier section. This will fill you up with energy.

Adjust the foam grip and assume a comfortable stance. The placement of the foam grip will vary according to the length of your arm.

The process of shooting the blowgun consists of nine steps. Steps (1) through (9) will take about 3 seconds.

1. Hold the blowgun at the foam grip with your right hand.
2. Using your left hand, drop the dart on the mouthpiece.
3. Push the dart (with either your thumb or index finger) so that its tail is flush with the breech.
4. Place your thumb on the breech to cover it (Figure 9-2).
5. Inhale.
6. Remove your thumb from the breech then place it below the blowgun to touch your ring finger.
7. Hold your breath as you center your mouth on the mouthpiece. If your blowgun does not have a mouthpiece, make sure there is a complete seal (Figure 9-3).
8. Depress (lower) the muzzle to aim the blowgun. Make sure that the muzzle of your blowgun is in the correct shooting configuration (Figure 9-11).
9. Blow.

FIGURE 9-2. The thumb placed on the breech for added safety

STANCE. I am right-handed and I find it comfortable to put my right foot in front when I hold the blowgun with my right hand in front (Figure 9-4). If you are not comfortable with this, try other stances. My right foot forward stance is a carry over from my stick fighting training.

Your knees must be straight. If your knees bend or unbend after you aim or as you blow air into the barrel, your dart will hit way off target.

It is not necessary for you to be standing when you shoot the blowgun. You can sit on a chair, on a log, on the floor, or on the ground. Standing or seated, you will be able to hit your target. Of course, you need to practice.

HOLDING. Hold the blowgun with your right hand (Figure 9-5) and with your left hand at the mouthpiece.

FIGURE 9-3 (above). You must ensure that there is a good seal when you shoot a blowgun that has no mouthpiece.

FIGURE 9-4 (right). My stance with my right foot in front

Most shooters support the barrel in the palm of their forward hand (Figure 9-6). In my case, I support the barrel placing the foam grip in the "V" formed by my thumb and index finger with my palm down. In this manner, I find it easier to use my index finger as a pointer when I aim the blowgun.

With your right hand on the foam grip (if the blowgun has one), hold the mouthpiece (in your left hand) between your ring and middle fingers (Figure 9-7). After pressing the mouthpiece to your mouth, place your thumb under the barrel touching your ring finger.

LOADING. Loading is a two-step process. Using your left hand, drop the tip of the dart into the barrel. Avoid hitting the mouthpiece.

FIGURE 9-5. Hold the blowgun with your right hand with your palm down. Place the barrel in the "V" formed by your thumb and index finger.

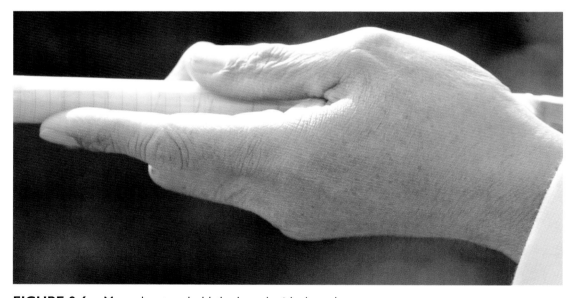

FIGURE 9-6. Many shooters hold the barrel with the palm up.

With the blowgun tilted slightly upward, load the dart then push the cone past the safety ring into the barrel (Figure 9-2). Then place your thumb under the barrel touching your ring finger.

INHALING. Inhale through your nose. Hold the mouthpiece a distance away from your mouth to avoid inhaling the dart although commercial blowguns have provisions for this. Do not inhale too much air. If you do, you will tend to blow prematurely. This will result in inaccurate hits. With experience, you will inhale just the right amount of air.

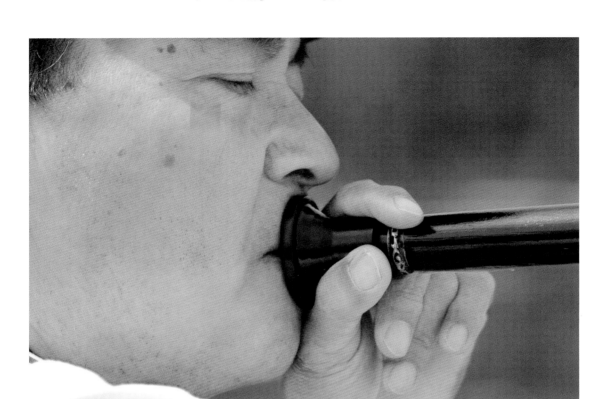

FIGURE 9-7. Hold the mouthpiece with your left hand. The barrel should be between your middle and index fingers.

FIGURE 9-8 (right, top). Loading a cone dart at the breech.
(right, bottom) Loading a bead dart at the muzzle. Drop the dart, bead first into the muzzle.

I inhale through my nose when I shoot the .40 caliber blowgun. However, when I shoot the .50 and .625 caliber blowguns, I inhale through my mouth. I experience tightness in my chest when I inhale through my nose when I use the higher caliber blowguns. However, I keep my thumb over the breech (Figure 9-2) when I inhale to avoid inhaling a dart. I remove it only after I complete my inhale.

Aiming. You cannot aim on a straight line and hit the target. You have to aim higher than your line of sight (Figure 9-9).

You will find it easy to align the tip of the blowgun so it would be on the correct horizontal left/right position (windage). The left/right placement of the tip of the blowgun will be determined by which of your eye is dominant and also by wind conditions. In still air, I "touch" the bull's-eye with the tip of the blowgun while keeping the bull's-eye slightly to the right.

The vertical up/down alignment (elevation) or angle of launch is more difficult to maintain. Place the bull's-eye below the tip of your blowgun to compensate for the pull of gravity and air resistance.

The placement of the tip of the blowgun in relation to the bull's-eye is what I call the *aiming configuration* (Figure 9-11).

The aiming configuration is the relative position formed by the tip of the blowgun with the bull's-eye. The correct aiming configuration can only be acquired by trial and error. After many trials and many shooting sessions, you would have imprinted the aiming configuration in your mind. At such time, you will be aiming instinctively. However, no matter how good a shot you have become, you will still occasionally make a particularly bad shot. If you do, you have to consciously correct your aim.

Do not make the mistake of shifting your eye away from the bull's-eye to the tip of your blowgun and back to the bull's-eye. If you do, you will experience some dizziness. Though it lasts only a fraction of a second, it could throw off your aim.

Fixing the eye on the target is the basic aiming method. Do not remove your eye from the target when you get darts from the cup to avoid the short-duration dizziness. However, during winter, if you wear gloves, you will need to look at the dart you are getting from the cup.

FIGURE 9-9. The tip of the blowgun should be slightly above the line of sight to compensate for the pull of gravity. The smaller the angle (*a*) between the line of sight and the tip of the blowgun the more accurate the shot will be. However, you need to blow harder to give the dart greater velocity.

When you are not comfortable with your aim, take your eyes off the target, point the blow-gun skyward, move your mouth away from the mouthpiece and take a deep breath—through your nose. Then go through your aiming motions again. Do not rush your shots. It takes about three seconds to load, aim, and shoot the blowgun. Taking too much time to aim will result in bad scores. Likewise, a hurried shot could also result in an errant dart.

BLOWING. Inhaling deeply then exhaling vigorously into the mouthpiece might not give you the best result. It can be harmful to your health. Also, too much air might choke the entrance to the barrel. This would result in air backing up and brushing against your cheeks. Avoid pushing the mouthpiece with your cheek as you blow, as this would spoil your aim.

When you blow, there will be some movement in your hands. Excessive movement will cause your aim to err. Do not move your head forward when you blow. This will also spoil your aim.

FOLLOW THROUGH. Follow through does not require motion. Indeed, you have to keep your posture until you see or hear the dart hit. Do not move too soon. You might move your blowgun even before the dart clears the muzzle.

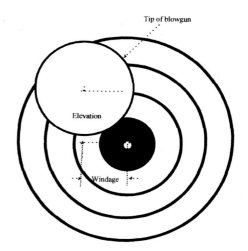

FIGURE 9-10. This illustrates the concept of the aiming configuration.

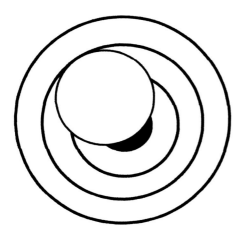

A. My actual aiming configuration shooting a one-piece .50 caliber blowgun using steel darts from 33 feet.

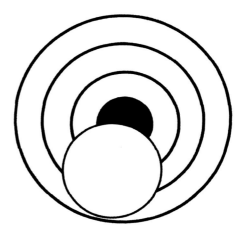

B. My actual aiming configuration shooting a three-piece .51 caliber blowgun using fukiya darts from 33 feet.

FIGURE 9-11. Aiming configuration: you will find that adjustment for windage seems instinctive. The elevation will depend on the distance you are shooting from and the velocity with which you can propel the dart. Aiming configuration B will look strange where the tip of the blowgun is lower than the bull's-eye. However, it results from the curvature of the three-piece .51 caliber blowgun (I use) giving the fukiya dart a tendency to shoot high.

chapter 10

FACTORS THAT WILL AFFECT YOUR AIM

Several factors will affect your aim. These will include your eyesight, the condition of your blowgun, the structure of your darts, the need to practice more, the environment, water inside the blowgun, and your concentration.

YOUR EYESIGHT

If you have good eyesight or are wearing corrective glasses, you will be able to see the bull's-eye from 33, 40, 50, or even from 100 feet. Whatever the condition of your eyes, your aim will be influenced by your dominant eye.

I am right-eye dominant. For this reason, I aim "more" with my right eye. Thus, I have a tendency to put the tip of my blowgun to the left of the bull's-eye. (See Figure 9-11.) I have a left-eye dominant student who puts the tip of his blowgun to the right of the bull's-eye. How can you tell which of your eye is dominant?

Stand on the spot from which you are to blow your dart at the target. Form a circle with your index fingers and thumbs (Figure 10-1). Hold the circle about a foot in front of your eye. With both eyes open, look through the circle and put the bull's-eye in the center.

Close your left eye. If the target remains in the circle, your right eye is dominant. To confirm, open your left eye and close your right eye. If your right eye is dominant, the target will move out of the circle.

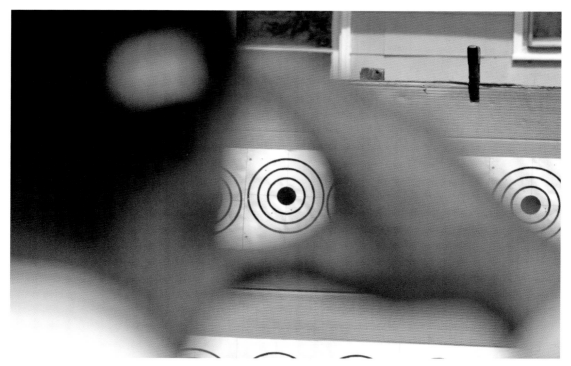

FIGURE 10-1. Forming the circle to determine which of your eye is dominant.

YOUR BLOWGUN

STRAIGHTNESS. Most short blowguns come as one piece. Longer blowguns come in two- or three-piece short sections.

Blowguns made from short lengths (under 6 feet) of copper, aluminum, or steel are rigid and normally straight. However, those made from PVC, unless encased in a rigid outer tube, are not.

Blowguns that consist of 2 or 3 short tubes with total lengths of less than six feet are also normally straight. However, after assembly, you will have to make sure that there is no gap where the short tubes meet and that the blowgun is straight.

As a precaution blow through the barrel to ensure that there is no dart in it. Look up the barrel against the sky. If you do not see a complete circle, rotate the barrel until you see one. Mark the top of the barrel with yellow tape or with ink.

Shoot a few darts to test the fit. Hold the blowgun with the yellow tape on top each time you shoot. I normally shoot bead darts and homemade darts with one-piece blowguns.

I have seen Matis Indians (on public television) shoot their blowguns at birds perched high up on trees clearly outlined against the sky. One shot three darts at a bird and missed three times. The bird did not fly away, attesting to the silence of the streaking dart. After his third shot, the Matis Indian smiled and muttered, "My blowgun is not straight."

LENGTH. I feel comfortable shooting a 3-foot 5-inch blowgun from 33 feet, a 4-feet 5-inch blowgun from 40 feet, and a 60-inch blowgun from 50 feet.

I have a better average shooting a two-piece 4-foot 5-inch blowgun from 33 feet than shooting a 3-foot 5-inch blowgun from the same distance (Figure 12-3, Figure 12-4). However, a blowgun can only be so long before it becomes too heavy, becomes too inconvenient, or becomes curved.

A long multi-piece blowgun will give you the following problems.

- Most doors are only about 6½ foot tall. You have to be careful not to hit the door with the barrel. Hitting a door can jar the connection between the short sections.

    A gap between the short sections will result in a reduced velocity of the dart as it hits the front edge of a section.
- There is a good chance that you will hit the ground with the muzzle of the blowgun while loading the dart. Loading will not be easy even if you are over 6 feet tall. A longer loading time can cause you to lose focus.
- The blowgun will curve due to its own weight. You will not see a complete circle when you look up the barrel. Except if you aim directly overhead. You will need to compensate for the curve by aiming at a higher elevation.

All of the above could result in a less accurate shot, or, a complete miss.

DIAMETER OF THE TUBE. A blowgun with a bigger bore (higher caliber) is potentially more powerful than one with a smaller bore. However, a blowgun can only be as powerful as the shooter's lungs will allow.

I have tried shooting a needle feathered with cotton through a soft drink straw. I have also tried shooting homemade darts through homemade blowguns that have 7/16-inch and ½-inch bores. I have shot .40, .50, .51 and .625 caliber blowguns. Linear graphs of my average points per dart are shown in Section 12.

YOUR DARTS

COMMERCIAL VERSUS HOMEMADE DARTS. Of the first 17 homemade darts I shot, 3 veered off the target and I couldn't find them in the grass. This did not happen when I shot new commercial cone darts.

I hollowed out the back end of the wooden tails to simulate the empty space in a plastic tail cone. I had to make sure that the hollow was at the center of the tail. Obviously, I did not do it right. But there could be other reasons.

The wooden tails that I made were from an assortment of trees and shrubs. Hence, even if they were of the same length and of near-identical diameters, they have different weights. For example: A dry rattan tail is light compared to a tail made from a freshly cut branch of an apple tree. This only means that I have to blow harder when the tail is heavier or aim the blowgun at a higher elevation.

With the weights of the tails being different, shoot only one kind of wooden tail in any one shooting session.

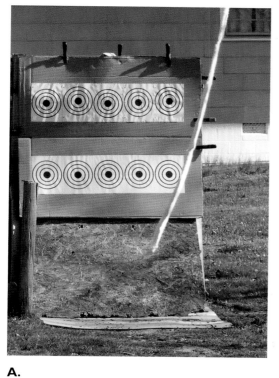

A.

B.

AA.

BB.

The .40 and .50 caliber darts are light and can be easily deflected off course by a 5 mph wind. The fukiya dart is light, presents a big lateral surface, and can easily be pushed even by a slight breeze. See Figure 12-12.

You will only see the tail cone of the dart as it streaks toward the target in still air. A 10-mph wind will push the tail cone and you will see the shaft being "wagged" by the wind. Figure 10-6 shows darts that hit the target at an angle caused by a slight breeze.

We can determine the effect of wind velocity on the dart if we know the velocity of the dart as it exits the blowgun.

The velocity of the dart as it exits the blowgun can be measured using a chronograph. The distance of the dart from the center of the bull's-eye can be measured with a ruler. Hence, we can even determine wind velocity. For example: If you are shooting from 33 feet with a blowgun that is 4 feet long, the dart will exit the blowgun 29 feet (33 – 4) from the target. If the dart exits the blowgun at 200 ft/sec (136.4 mph), and was pushed by the wind 2 inches from the center of the bull's-eye, we can determine the velocity of the wind. From Figure 10-7

$$\tan \theta = \frac{2/12}{29} = \frac{v_w}{200} \qquad (10\text{-}1)$$

A solution of (10-1) yields, vw = 1.2 ft/sec or 0.8 mph.

Wind that you can barely feel on your cheek will have a velocity of about 1 mph. A 1 mph wind will push the dart about 2.6 inches from the center of the bull's-eye. Thus, instead of scoring 5 points, you will score 3 points. A 5 mph (7.3 ft/sec) wind that hits a dart broadside will push it 12.8 inches from the center of the bull's-eye—a miss.

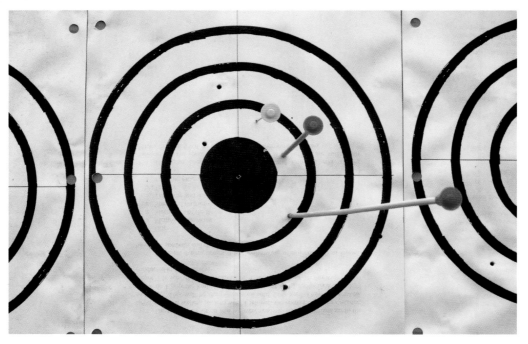

FIGURE 10-6. Darts pushed by the wind. You can hardly see the steel shaft of the dart at the top. The 6" bamboo shaft (center) was pushed by the wind slightly; the 12" bamboo shaft (bottom), sharply.

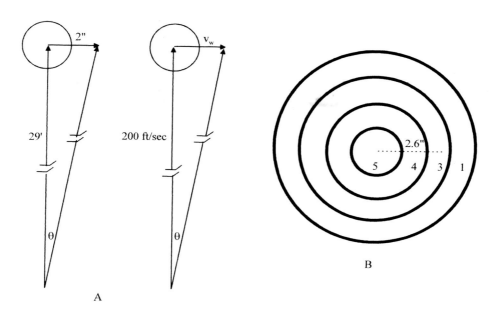

FIGURE 10-7. Effect of wind velocity on a dart. A 0.8 mph wind will push the dart 2 inches away from the center of the bull's-eye (A). A I mph wind will push the dart 2.6 inches away from the center of the bull's-eye. Thus, the dart will be scored 3 instead of 5 points (B).

In my yard, I am shielded from the wind by fences, neighbors' houses, shrubs, and trees. For this reason, if the wind blows at 5 mph, when it gets to me, its velocity could be down to 1 mph. But of course, to keep my average up, I wait for the wind to die down so I can shoot in still air.

LIGHTING. When you shoot indoors, your target must be well lighted. When you shoot outdoors, lighting will not be a problem except on a cloudy day.

TEMPERATURE. Make sure that you are dressed right. On a cold windy day, you will have low scores. On a nice day, all things being equal, you will have better scores.

Wear gloves and several layers of clothing to keep warm during winter. I have shot blowguns in temperatures as low as 20°F.

During summer, the temperature can hit as high as 99°F at noon. Shoot early in the day. In my backyard, a big tree gives me shade starting at about 3 PM.

SUN IN YOUR EYES. You will have to position your target so that your back or your side will be toward the sun. Even so, the sun's glare could be bothersome.

Sunglasses such as those used in handgun or rifle shooting will help reduce glare and will give a sharper image of the target.

MOISTURE IN THE AIR. On a particularly cold and humid day, there will be pockets of air with different densities. When your dart hits these pockets, it could veer off unpredictably.

When there is a slight drizzle, you might try to shoot through the raindrops. I have, but with mixed frustration and elation.

WATER INSIDE THE BLOWGUN

If you have a cup of coffee, tea, chocolate, or soda just before you shoot, your breath will be laden with moisture.

You will be surprised at how fast water will condense in the barrel of your blowgun. During summer, water vapor from your breath will stay as vapor. However, during winter and during days of high humidity, water vapor will condense in the barrel. You might even see water spray coming out with your dart. Your darts will even carry water to your target!

During the warm months, water in the barrel will cause your aim to err only a little. Your dart will streak "squiggly" into your target but will still hit close enough to the bull's-eye. You can whisk the water off by swinging the barrel but only with a one-piece blowgun. Should you do this, do not jerk the barrel as you might cause it to curve. There is a better way, though.

Tie a cotton cloth with a twine that is at least 12" longer than your blowgun (Figure 16-1). Thread the end of the twine through a small bead. To remove moisture from inside the barrel, drop the bead through the bore. As it clears the muzzle, pull the bead and the cleaning cloth through the barrel several times to remove the water.

CONCENTRATION

Shooting indoors or in still air is much different from shooting outdoors. Outdoors, the sun could be in your eyes and the wind could be blowing. Both could result in physical discomfort and in a low shooting average.

You have to load quickly and shoot as fast. Taking too much time to aim can fill your mind with extraneous thoughts. You must keep your focus so that each time you shoot your blowgun is in the correct aiming configuration.

Even the shooting of only 10 darts can cause you to lose focus. When your attention waivers, pause momentarily then resume shooting.

BIRDS, BUGS, AND NEIGHBORS. Other factors could affect your concentration. I've had bugs prancing in front of my eyes, a robin searching for earthworms, a starling flying between me and my target, a mosquito buzzing my ears, a ladybug walking on the barrel of my blowgun, a bug using my sunglasses as a landing pad, and a squirrel running atop a fence.

Smoke from cigarettes, noise from lawn mowers, a dog or a car suddenly coming into view are also distractions. Worst are exhaust gases from passing cars.

FATIGUE. Fatigue can also set in. If you shoot, say, 200 light darts (.40 caliber, .50 caliber, or the .51 caliber fukiya dart) take a short break.

Shooting the .625 caliber dart is a different matter. After each three shots, I have to take a short pause and really focus because I've run out of breath!

chapter 11

KEEPING SCORE

If you shoot darts occasionally, you might be satisfied with merely sticking the darts. However, if you take the shooting of darts seriously, you might want to track your progress. You can count the number of darts that hit the target. You can rely on memory to keep track of yesterday's count as compared to today's performance. However, your memory will soon fail you. It is better to record your hits and misses.

All your darts might hit the target. However, one dart might be at one corner of your target and the other, say, several inches away. Hence, no matter how studiously you keep count, this will only give you an approximate measure of your skill.

There must be some way to quantitatively track your progress.

GROUPING

With continued practice, you will be able to bunch your shots with the two farthest darts only fractions of an inch away from each other. You can measure the distance between the two farthest darts and keep a record of such measurements. Obviously, the closer you can bunch or group your shots, the better shot you are. However, it is very likely that you will put holes on or render useless a good number of tail cones.

Grouping is a good way of measuring consistency. That is, you are able to place your darts in a relatively small area. However, if you use grouping to keep track of your progress, you have to consider the following:

- You need to bring a ruler to your target area.
- You might become more concerned with the relative distances between the darts—not with hitting the bull's-eye.
- No matter how infrequent, how would you measure a dart that completely missed the target, the one that missed the side of the barn?
- If you shoot 500 darts a day, when will you measure a group? After each five, ten, or fifteen shots? The less the number of darts in a group the more times you have to use a ruler.
- You could damage the darts.

As a measure of skill, one will have to be both accurate and consistent. For example: Consider Figure 11-1. Shooter A is consistent. His darts are in a close group that measures 2 inches. But he completely missed the bull's-eye. Shooter B's group measures 3 inches. But he is more accurate. Four of his darts hit the bull's-eye. Hence, a shooter can be consistent but he might not be accurate.

Grouping is one way of tracking one's progress. However, there is a better way of tracking the development of your skill—one that will refer a group to a given target—the bull's-eye.

SCORING EACH DART

A better way of measuring consistency and accuracy can be had by adopting a system of scoring not unlike the method used in archery. Here is how it works.

FIGURE 11-1. A blowgun shooter might be consistent but he might not be accurate. Here, shooter A's grouping (left) is better than that of Shooter B (right). However, shooter B hit the bull's-eye 4 times. Shooter A did not.

Make a target consisting of a set of concentric circles, with 2, 4, 6, and 8 inch diameters (Figure 11-2). The center circle is the bull's-eye. Assign points to a dart that hits a given area. For example: A dart that hits the bull's-eye gets 5 points; the 4 inch circle, 4 points; the 6 inch circle, 3 points; and the 8 inch circle, 1 point. Any dart that hits a line will be scored the higher point.

You can hit the bull's-eye and score a perfect 5 points. Obviously, if you are shooting at an average of 2 points per dart, there is a lot of room for improvement. An average of 3.5 points per dart, shooting from 40 feet using a 4-foot 5-inch blowgun, is excellent. The method of calculations is straightforward. A sample calculation is given in Appendix H.

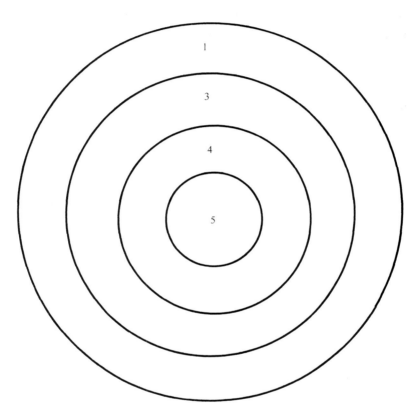

FIGURE 11-2. Points assigned for hits. An incoming dart that gets embedded on an already-embedded dart is given the same score.

chapter 12

MEASURING THE SHOOTER'S SKILL

There are three ways of measuring a shooter's skill. The first two are ideal for the solitary shooter. The third is the one used in competitions.

1. The shooter's average can be plotted against time. The linear graph generated is the learning curve that is very useful in comparing the various caliber/length/distance/dart mix. The learning curve shows at a glance the rate at which the shooter is learning.
2. The total number of times the shooter hits the target circles are plotted and the resulting column graph displays the number of times the shooter hits the bull's-eye and the other circles of lesser points.
3. The shooter's total number of points is tabulated. This is a method of scoring that is used in competitions where the shooter with the highest score wins.

LEARNING CURVE

The learning of any motor skill, such as the shooting of a dart, can be modeled by what is called a learning curve. This curve will show that learning comes quickly at first but eventually levels off and approaches a limiting value. This limiting value is the upper limit of the shooter's accuracy.

Once you reach the upper limit of your accuracy, you would have reached the point of diminishing returns. At this point, you could be shooting thousands of darts but with little improvement in your shooting average. Thus, the learning curve will tell you when to stop shooting the particular blowgun/dart/distance/caliber mix. However, if you want to continue shooting, you can do so from a farther distance, or use a different caliber blowgun, or use a different dart.

The reader will probably ask the following questions:

1. Which caliber blowgun should I shoot?
2. How would you compare the accuracy of blowguns with the same length shot from different distances?
3. How would you compare the accuracy of blowguns of different lengths?
4. Which is more accurate to shoot, a cone or bead dart?
5. Is a dart with a longer shaft more accurate than one with a shorter shaft?
6. Which is more accurate, a .40 caliber, a .50 caliber, or a .625 caliber blowgun?

These questions will be answered but first let me put time lines on the learning curves illustrated.

I had two operations on each eye. Before my eye operations, I wore corrective glasses and shot, exclusively .40 caliber blowguns. After my eye operations I had 20/20 vision and shot .50, .51, and .625 caliber blowguns.

Recently, I decided to shoot the .40 caliber blowgun again to compare my shooting averages before and after my eye operations. I plotted my learning curve and found that I really am shooting better now. However, I felt that a "before and after eye operations" graph would only be of interest to me and for this reason did not include it here.

SHOOTING THE SAME BLOWGUN USING THE SAME DARTS FROM DIFFERENT DISTANCES

The first line graphs I generated were my average points per dart shooting a one-piece, .40 caliber, 3-foot 5-inch blowgun from 33 feet and from 40 feet (Figure 12-1). Hence, in essence, this graph is part of my learning curve for all the other line graphs I generated afterward. All my subsequent learning curves were shortened by these learning curves.

The steepest portions of the two line graphs are in the first 3 months. This is where I developed a good stance, figured out my aiming configuration, became consistent with the mechanics of shooting, and developed the ability to focus on the target. These are all explained in Section 10.

TABLE 12-1. Values plotted in Figure 12-1.

Month #	33'	40'
1	2.96	2.91
2	3.20	3.13
3	3.38	3.22
4	3.43	3.28
5	3.46	3.28
6	3.52	3.37
7	3.56	3.39
8	3.59	3.40
9	3.61	3.42
10	3.67	3.47
11	3.68	3.53
12	3.69	3.54

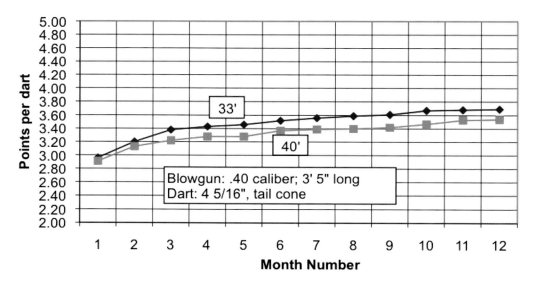

FIGURE 12-1. Learning curves for shooting the same blowgun using the same darts from different distances. (In this and the other graphs following, unless otherwise specified, each line represents 36,500 shots. Thus, for this graph, I shot 73,000 darts.)

Figure 12-1 is a quantitative proof of the common experience that the closer you are to the target, the more accurate you will be.

Similarly, I generated Figure 12-2 shooting 100 darts from 40 feet and 50 feet every day for the equivalent of a 12-month period. However, in this case, I used a longer blowgun.

TABLE 12-2. Values plotted in Figure 12-2.

Month #	50'	40'
1	3.66	3.73
2	3.72	3.80
3	3.73	3.83
4	3.74	3.85
5	3.74	3.86
6	3.75	3.87
7	3.75	3.87
8	3.76	3.87
9	3.77	3.88
10	3.76	3.90
11	3.77	3.90
12	3.78	3.92

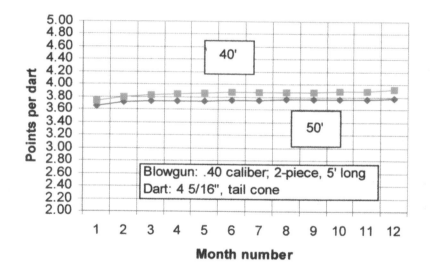

FIGURE 12-2. Learning curves for shooting a 60-inch blowgun using the same darts from 40 and 50 feet.

SHOOTING BLOWGUNS WITH DIFFERENT LENGTHS FROM THE SAME DISTANCE

Shooting the different distance-caliber-dart mix did not happen in the same 12-month periods. Indeed, the time elapsed (the ordinate Month number) are not necessarily consecutive months. Sometimes, month number two could be in March and month number three in June of the same year. For example: I shot the 4-foot 5-inch blowgun from 33 feet later than I did the 3-foot 5-inch blowgun. Hence, while Figure 12-3A is a good way of comparing accuracy shooting different length blowguns from the same distance, Figure 12-3B reflects a better reality.

Figure 12-3A is a graphic presentation of the common experience that a shooter will have a better average shooting a longer blowgun. Figure 12-3B illustrates that my learning curve for shooting the 4-foot 5-inch blowgun was shortened by my learning curve for shooting the 3-inch 5-inch blowgun.

Figure 12-4 further illustrates that the shooter will be more accurate shooting a longer blowgun.

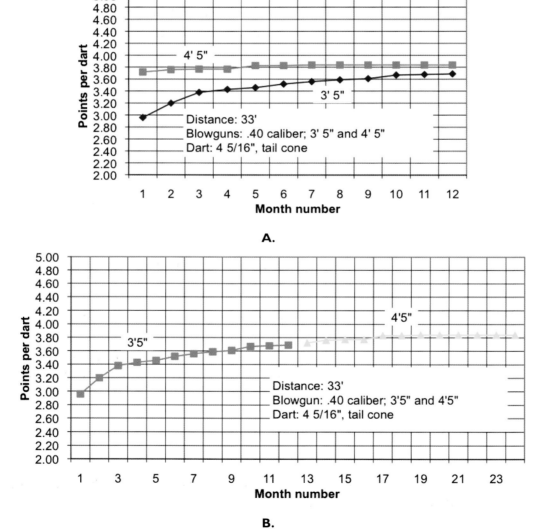

FIGURE 12-3. Two representations of the learning curves for shooting blowguns with different lengths from the same distance.

TABLE 12-3. Values plotted in Figure 12-4.

Month #	5'	4' 5"	3' 5"
1	3.73	3.23	2.91
2	3.80	3.42	3.13
3	3.83	3.46	3.22
4	3.85	3.49	3.28
5	3.86	3.51	3.28
6	3.87	3.54	3.37
7	3.87	3.58	3.39
8	3.87	3.54	3.40
9	3.88	3.66	3.42
10	3.90	3.69	3.47
11	3.90	3.73	3.53
12	3.92	3.74	3.54

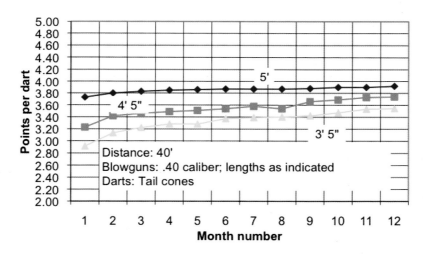

FIGURE 12-4. Learning curves for shooting blowguns with different lengths from 40'.

SHOOTING THE SAME BLOWGUN FROM THE SAME DISTANCE USING CONE AND BEAD DARTS

Cone and bead darts have very different shapes. Hence, one will expect that there will be a difference in shooting averages. Indeed, there is.

- The cone dart is breech-loaded; the bead dart, muzzle-loaded. Thus, it takes longer to load and shoot a bead dart.

- There is a greater tendency of a shaft separating from the bead compared to that of the shaft separating from the cone.
- An incoming dart can hit and become embedded in the tail cone of an already embedded dart. Thus, it can be scored the same as the dart it becomes embedded to.
- An incoming dart that hits a bead dart that is already embedded will bounce off and will have to be considered a miss. Thus, it has to be scored zero.
- There is an air trap in the cone dart. There is none in the bead dart. Thus, a greater velocity can be imparted to the tail cone dart.

The effect of these variables on my accuracy shooting the bead dart is shown in Figure 12-5.

My rate of learning shooting the tail cone and the bead dart are almost identical in the first 4 months. However, in the 12th month, I averaged 3.69 for the cone dart and only 3.47 for the bead dart. Thus, I am less accurate shooting the bead dart.

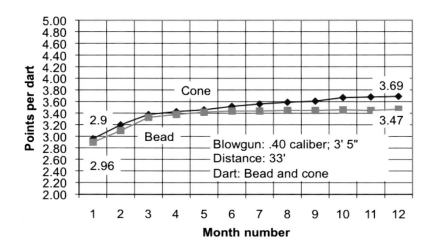

FIGURE 12-5. Learning curves for shooting bead and cone darts using the same blowgun from a common distance of 33 feet.

SHOOTING THE SAME BLOWGUN FROM THE SAME DISTANCE USING CONE DARTS WITH SHAFTS OF DIFFERENT LENGTHS

I assumed that I would be more accurate shooting a longer dart before I decided to generate this graph. I was right, but not by much. I was only slightly more accurate shooting the longer 5-inch dart (Figure 12-6).

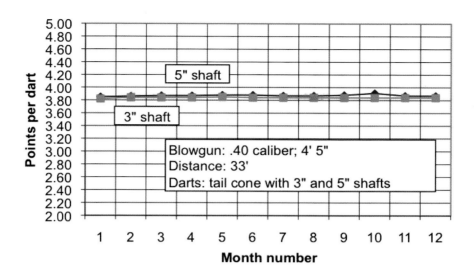

FIGURE 12-6. Learning curves for shooting steel shafts of different lengths.

SHOOTING BLOWGUNS WITH DIFFERENT BORES FROM THE SAME DISTANCE

I shot the .40 caliber blowgun more than 500,000 times before I started shooting the .625 caliber blowgun. Hence, I (my lungs) was used to blowing ".40-caliber quantity air" through the .40 caliber blowgun. I was not prepared for my first shot using the .625 caliber blowgun. My dart hit three feet below my target!

The bore of the .625 caliber blowgun is 1.67 times bigger than that of the .40 caliber blowgun (Figure 12-7). Hence, one would have to blow more air into the .625 caliber blowgun if he expects to propel a dart with the same velocity as in the .40 caliber blowgun. Earlier, in Section 6, the required volumetric flow rate was calculated to be $V6 = 2.8V4$ (Figure 12-8). This ratio only partly explains why I missed so badly.

The dart used in the .625 caliber blowgun is 3 times heavier than that used in the .40 caliber blowgun. The effect of the weight difference of the darts on the average force required to propel it is given in Equation 6-35.

Looking at Figure 12-9, it would seem that my learning curve for shooting the .625 caliber blowgun was not helped by the 500,000 darts I shot prior to it. It did help, however, as I

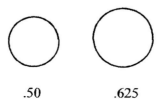

.50   .625

FIGURE 12-7. Actual sizes (also Figure 6-6) of the blowguns I used to generate the learning curves illustrated in Figure 12-11.

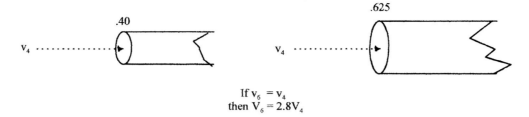

$$\text{If } v_6 = v_4$$
$$\text{then } V_6 = 2.8V_4$$

FIGURE 12-8 (also Figure 6-9).

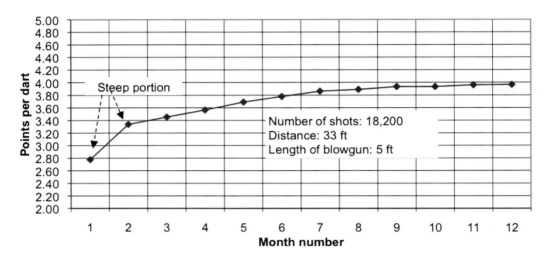

FIGURE 12-9. Learning curve for shooting the .625 caliber blowgun.

learned to assume the correct stance, to adjust the aiming configuration, and to develop a consistent mechanics of shooting. However, for the .625 caliber blowgun, I had to re-learn how to inhale and exhale the correct quantity of air.

The effect on my accuracy of the required increased volumetric flow rate (equation 6-19), the greater impulse (equation 6-35) required to push the dart through the .625 caliber blowgun and the need to re-learn how to inhale and exhale the correct quantity of air is apparent in the steep portion (the first two months) of my learning curve in Figure 12-9. However, despite my initial inconsistency, by Month nine I became consistently accurate.

The curve looks smooth but only because my average was plotted on a monthly basis. However, Figure 12-10 shows how erratic I was in my first 1,500 shots. I was more consistent in my next 1,500 shots then became more accurate and even more consistent in my last 1,400 shots.

Figure 12-11 illustrates my shooting averages for a .50 caliber and .625 caliber blowguns. A more accurate comparison can be had if the blowguns were of identical lengths and if the weights of the darts were the same.

A comparison of my shooting averages for the .50 caliber blowgun and that for the .625 blowgun will be like comparing apples and oranges. The weight of the darts I used with the .625 caliber blowgun is at least 3 times the weight of the darts I used with the .50 caliber blowgun.

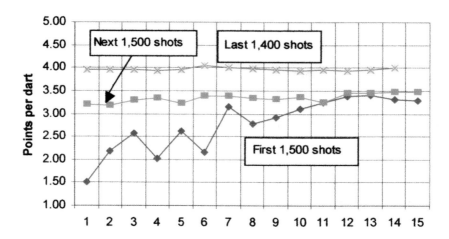

FIGURE 12-10. My learning curve comparing my first 1,500 shots to the next 1,500 shots then to the last 1,400 shots using the .625 caliber blowgun.

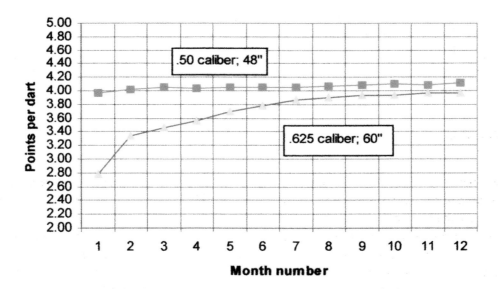

FIGURE 12-11. Learning curves for shooting .50 and a .625 caliber blowgun from a common distance of 33'. Each line represents 18,600 shots.

Figure 12-11 shows that I am less accurate with the .625 caliber blowgun. However, it would not be correct to attribute my being less accurate to the big bore of the .625 caliber blowgun. Rather, that *I need more time to practice with it and that I need a stronger pair of lungs*. Hence, I would advise the reader against using Figure 12-11 as a basis for buying his blowgun.

I am positive that the reader who has a stronger pair of lungs than mine would become more accurate shooting the .625 caliber blowgun in a shorter period of time.

It is not the blowgun that is more or less accurate than another – it is the shooter.

SHOOTING THE FUKIYA DART

Wind velocity has the most effect on the fukiya dart (Figure 12-12). A slight breeze will push it off course. However, the air trapped in the fukiya dart will contribute to its greater velocity inside the barrel. Thus, the shooter can aim the .51 caliber blowgun at a shallow angle that will make for a better aiming configuration (See Figure 9-11).

The relative lateral surfaces of 3 different darts are shown in Figure 12-12. The tail of the .40 caliber dart is ⅝-inch long with its cone ⅜-inch in diameter. The tail of the .50 caliber dart is a cone with a ½-inch diameter sitting on a cylinder that is ⁷⁄₁₆-inch long. The fukiya dart is about 8-inch long with a 0.51-inch diameter.

Fukiya darts can be shot accurately in still air. However, even a light breeze will push it off target and will lower your shooting average.

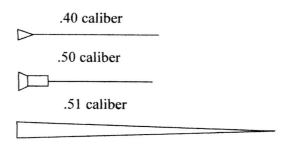

A. Relative lateral surfaces of 3 different darts. The .51 caliber fukiya dart is at the bottom.

B. At left is one fukiya dart inside another. The darts were shot from 33 feet.

FIGURE 12-12.

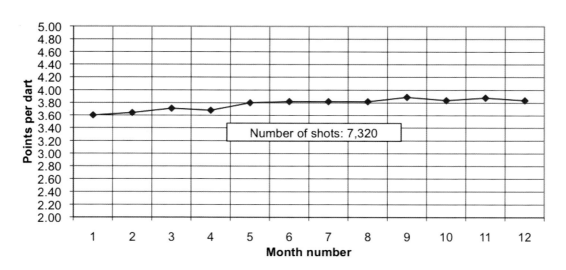

FIGURE 12-13. Learning curve for shooting .51 caliber fukiya darts.

The learning curve is a limited growth curve, that is, it has an upper limit that can only be approached but never reached (Figure 12-14).

The mathematical equation for the learning curve[10] is

$$y = a - be^{-rx} \qquad (12\text{-}1)$$

where e = 2.72.

At first glance, equation (12-1) seems too abstract to be associated with shooting the blowgun, but it is not. We can use equation (12-1) to determine the equation of *my* learning curve shown in Figure 12-15.

The maximum value for hitting the

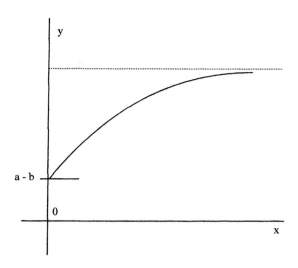

FIGURE 12-14. Learning curve.

bull's-eye is 5, that is, a = 5. My average for the first month is 2.96 points per dart (Table 12-4). Therefore a − b = 2.96, giving b = 2.04. Substituting these values into (12-1), we get

$$y = 5 - 2.04e^{-rx} \qquad (12\text{-}2)$$

Table 12-4 lists pairs of values of x (month number − 1) and y (points per dart). Hence, we can solve for r and find the equation for my shooting average. For example: With x = 1 and y = 3.20, equation 12-2 becomes

$$3.20 = 5 - 2.04e^{-r(1)}$$

Solving, we get r = 0.12. Thus, one of the equations for my learning curve shown in Figure 12-15 is

$$y = 5 - 2.04e^{-0.12x} \qquad (12\text{-}3)$$

However, for each pair of x and y, the computed values of r may or may not be the same as can be seen in the last column of Table 12-4. By trial, I found that the **best fit** is when r = 0.05 where x = 7 and y = 3.59. Therefore, the best equation for my learning curve as shown in Figure 12-15 is

$$y = 5 - 2.04e^{-0.05x} \qquad (12\text{-}4)$$

To check how close the values are, equation (12-4) is plotted against my actual average in Figure 12-16.

Table 12-4. My average shooting the .40 caliber 3-foot 5-inch blowgun from 33 feet.

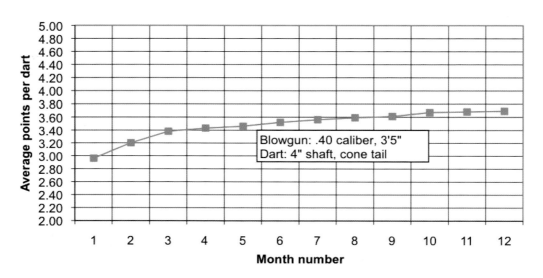

FIGURE 12-15. Learning curve for shooting the .40 caliber 3-inch5-inch blowgun from 33 feet.

TABLE 12-4. My average shooting the .40 caliber 3-foot 5-inch blowgun from 33 feet.

Month Number	x	y (Actual)	r (computed)
1	0	2.96	
2	1	3.20	0.12
3	2	3.38	0.12
4	3	3.43	0.09
5	4	3.46	0.07
6	5	3.52	0.07
7	6	3.56	0.06
8	7	3.59	0.05
9	8	3.61	0.05
10	9	3.67	0.03
11	10	3.68	0.03
12	11	3.69	0.02

TABLE 12-5. Theoretical values of y when r = 0.05.

Month Number	x	rx	e^{rx}	$2.04/e^{rx}$	Theoretical $y=5-2.04/e^{rx}$	Actual y
1	0	0	1	2.04	2.96	2.96
2	1	0.05	1.05	1.94	3.06	3.20
3	2	0.10	1.11	1.85	3.15	3.38
4	3	0.15	1.16	1.76	3.24	3.43
5	4	0.20	1.22	1.67	3.33	3.46
6	5	0.25	1.28	1.59	3.41	3.52
7	6	0.30	1.35	1.51	3.49	3.56
8	7	0.35	1.42	1.44	3.56	3.59
9	8	0.40	1.49	1.37	3.63	3.61
10	9	0.45	1.57	1.30	3.70	3.67
11	10	0.50	1.65	1.24	3.76	3.68
12	11	0.55	1.73	1.18	3.82	3.69

COLUMN GRAPH

A good measure of skill, aside from the average points per dart, is the number of times the shooter is able to hit the bull's-eye. In this case, instead of the usual learning curve, the number of times the darts hit inside the 2, 4, 6, and 8 inch circles is plotted as a column graph. Figure 12-17 shows, at a glance, that I hit the bull's-eye 5,613 times in 18,600 tries, a ratio of 1:3.3. I hit the bull's-eye at better than 1 in 4 shots.

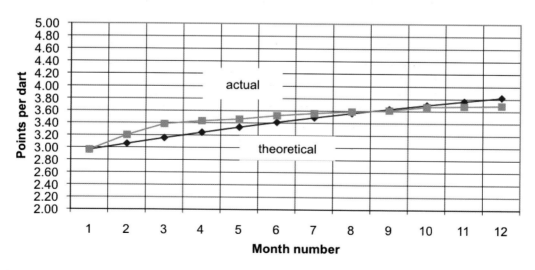

FIGURE 12-16. A comparison of the theoretical (y = 5 – 2.04e-0.05x) and my actual average shooting the .40 caliber 3-foot 5-inch blowgun from 33 feet.

The column graph can also be used to compare darts. For example: Figure 12-19 compares the number of times I hit the target circles using a bamboo dart and a steel dart. (See also Figure 12-20.) Figure 12-19 shows that I hit the bull's-eye more often when I used steel darts.

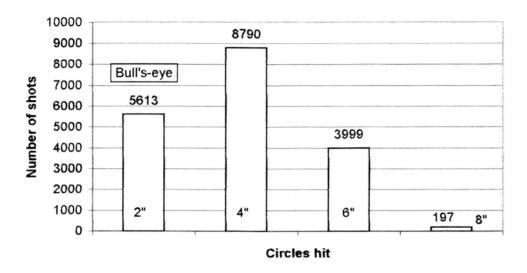

FIGURE 12-17. Column graph showing circles hit shooting cone tail darts with steel shafts through a .50 caliber blowgun.

SHOOTING BAMBOO DARTS VERSUS SHOOTING STEEL DARTS

A bamboo shaft will have an unavoidable curve. A bamboo dart has a greater lateral surface than a dart with a steel shaft. Hence, wind velocity will affect its trajectory more than it would a dart with a steel shaft. Indeed, even in still air, sometimes a bamboo dart could veer off sharply. These will result in a lower shooting average.

The steel shaft is sharper and has a much smaller diameter than a bamboo shaft. Hence, the steel shaft will penetrate more deeply into the target. The bamboo dart will also penetrate a cardboard target but sometimes the impact of a second dart could jar an already embedded bamboo dart and cause it to pop out of the target. If you are keeping score, you might need to re-shoot the dart that popped out.

The bamboo dart, although not as sharp as the steel dart, could also penetrate the tail of an already embedded dart and put a big hole in it (Figure 8-3) thereby rendering it useless.

I had to wait until no wind was blowing before I shot the bamboo and steel darts. However, oftentimes, the wind would pick up speed as the dart exited the blowgun. In one such shoot, the wind was blowing toward me. As a result, one dart stalled and hit flat. Two other darts completely missed the target.

Figure 12-19 shows the number of times I hit the bull's-eye and the other circles. There is a marked difference between my shooting averages for the two darts.

In Figure 12-6, there is not much difference between my averages for shooting 3" and 5" steel darts. This only means that I was able to make the correct change in my aiming configuration.

However, I felt that it would be more difficult to make the correct change in my aiming configuration if the difference in the lengths (and weights) of the darts were greater. To find out, I shot bamboo darts where one is 6" longer and therefore a lot heavier than the other. A comparison is shown in Figure 12-20.

If you are to interpret Figure 12-20, it will help to look back at the factors that will affect your aim (Section 10). In this instance, the two darts are shot from the same distance using a blowgun of the same caliber and length. With this and the assumption that in each case the darts are shot with the correct aiming configuration, one would think that he would be equally accurate with the two darts. Not quite. Figure 12-20 shows that I am more accurate with the 6-inch dart. I hit the bull's-eye more often.

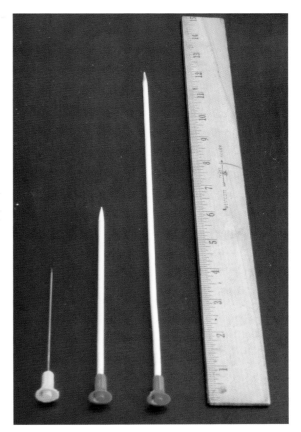

FIGURE 12-18. Steel and bamboo darts (left and center) used to generate Figure 12-19 and bamboo darts (center and right) used to generate Figure 12-20.

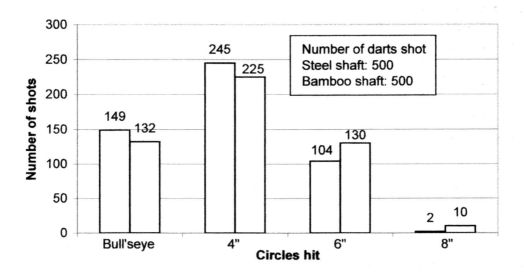

FIGURE 12-19. Comparison of shots using .50 caliber darts with steel (left bar) and bamboo (right bar) shafts.

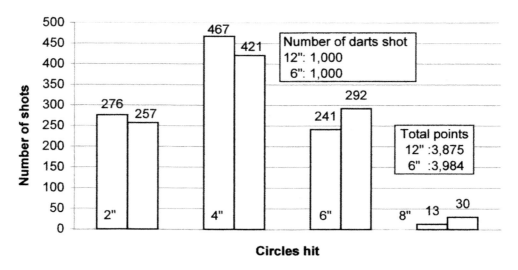

FIGURE 12-20. Column graph for shooting 6-inch (left bar) and 12-inch (right bar) bamboo darts from 33 feet using a .50 caliber blowgun.

One critical factor that could escape the shooter's attention is the straightness of the darts. The longer 12-inch dart will likely have a more pronounced curve than the shorter 6-inch dart. Hence, you will be less accurate shooting the 12-inch dart.

What you could do is to have a set of 20 darts that you should test-shoot. You will find that even in still air, there will be darts that would veer off sharply. Indeed, you can easily miss a 4 by 3 foot target if your dart is curved and if there is a slight wind. Set aside the darts that hit wide of your target. Use only the darts that shoot straight.

At this point, the reader would have developed admiration not only for the skill of blowgun hunters but also for their skill in making blowguns and darts that shoot straight. Let us not forget, too, their tracking skills.

TOTAL POINTS SCORED

The shooter could shoot any number of darts in his backyard when practicing alone. However, when he shoots with a friend, they might decide to keep score to see who the better shot is. In this case, the number of shots can be agreed on and the scores totaled afterward. A score sheet that can be used to record the hits for such a backyard shoot is shown in Table 12-6. (See also Appendix B.)

It is best to break up the shoot into rounds to avoid the contest from dragging on. For example: A shooter will be required to shoot 5 darts each in 6 rounds. Thus, each will shoot 30 darts after which the score is totaled and the winner is determined.

Table 12-7 shows a shooter's score in one round. A perfect shot would be when a shooter hits the bull's-eye. For this round, the shooter scored 21 points out of a possible 25 points.

TABLE 12-6. Competition Score Sheet.

Shooter A	Round		
Target, circles	Number of sticks	Points	Total
Inside 2 inches	2	5	10
4 inches	2	4	8
6 inches	1	3	3
8 inches	0	1	0
Outside 8 inches	0	0	0
Total			21

TABLE 12-7. Score Sheet for One Round.

Shooter A	Round		
Target, circles	Number of sticks	Points	Total
Inside 2 inches		5	
4 inches		4	
6 inches		3	
8 inches		1	
Outside 8 inches		0	
Total			

The number of rounds and the number of darts shot per round are designed to eliminate the element of luck. The total scores will be a good measure of the shooters' relative skills.

chapter 13

THE BLOWGUN AS A HUNTER'S WEAPON

In the sporting use of the blowgun, there are rules to follow. The shooter has to shoot from a given distance, use a blowgun with a given length and caliber, and shoot darts with specific dimensions. In a tournament or in a friendly contest, after shooting a given number of darts, the scores are totaled and the winner is declared.

In the use of the blowgun as a weapon or for hunting, there are no rules to follow. The distance is variable for the target does not hold still. The blowgun is as long and as heavy as the shooter can carry. The darts are either ready to be loaded or are feathered during the hunt. No scores are kept. But the "winner" is the hunter who brings down the game.

The most documented and perhaps the most studied blowgun hunters are the Ecuadorians. Two scholars who lived with them to study their way of life gave first hand accounts of the Ecuadorians' skill as blowgun hunters. One was Philippe Descola,[11] who authored *Life and Death in The Amazon: The Spears of Twilight*; the other was John Man,[3] who wrote *Jungle Nomads of Ecuador: The Waorani*. Birds were not the only targets. The Ecuadorians aimed primarily at the woolly monkey that lived high up in the trees of the Amazon.

Philippe Descola, in a hunting trip with a Capahuari described, "Pinchu slots a dart into his blowpipe... Throwing his head back and holding the heavy blowpipe completely vertical, Pinchu has now silently blown his first dart and immediately reloads."

John Man, in as much detail, described his hunting trip with the Waorani Kadowae. Man writes, "... he quickly loaded his blowgun and raised it to his mouth. Filling his lungs with air, he then blew so hard that his whole body seemed to explode with the release of tension."

On the other side of the Pacific, in Indonesia, Malaysia, and the Philippines, similar hunting scenes were taking place. However, instead of fashioning their blowguns from the chonta tree, they made it from bamboo. The Indonesians shot small game with the sumpitan while the Filipinos used sumpits. In Japan, the blowgun was used to hunt birds in the Edo era. The Japanese word torisashi means to stick birds with a blowgun. Strangely, although bamboo also grows in Japan, there is no record of it being used to make blowguns.

In the United States, modern backwoodsmen[12] have used the blowgun for fishing and for hunting small game such as birds, rabbits, and squirrels. The Cherokees who are well known for their skill aimed their blowguns at small game such as squirrels.

FIGURE 13-1. The squirrel had been one of the main targets of the blowgun as evidenced by the many recipes given in old cookbooks (in the US). It is said that it can be substituted for chicken in recipes. A squirrel can easily measure 8" (from its nose to its behind) by 3" (the width of its body) and thus can easily fill a standard target that consists of circles that have 2", 4", 6" and 8" diameters.

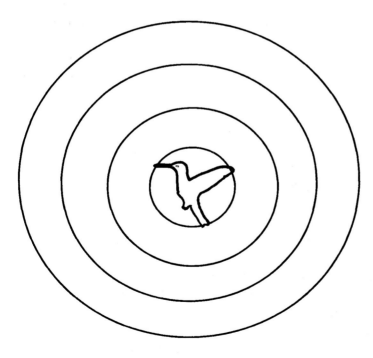

FIGURE 13-2. The Virginia hummingbird weighs about 0.106 oz and has a length of 3.5 – 4 inches. The smallest bird in the world is the bee hummingbird,[5] which weighs 0.06 oz and measures about 2 inches and can be found in South America. This should explain the legend about the Jivaros shooting hummingbirds from 50 yards.

chapter 14

THE BLOWGUN AS A DEFENSIVE WEAPON

The use of a blowgun against an enemy is obvious. It can be shot from ambush after which the shooter can escape unnoticed. In such an ambush, the shooter can carry as a long a blowgun as he wants. However, short blowguns such as those used in the Chinese martial arts require different tactics.

The two blowguns in the Chinese martial arts are considered hidden weapons.

1. The mea hua needle made from goose feathers is only 2 inches long and shoots a 1½-inch dart.
2. The blowing arrow made from bamboo is only 6 inches long and shoots a 5-inch bamboo dart.

A dozen mea hua needles can be carried "up the sleeve" unnoticed. It is even impossible to detect when used in the dark. However, it is not separate from but an integral part of empty hand techniques. One such instance of its use against several robbers by a lady master of the mea hua needle, Ming Nuan, was described in Douglas Hsieh's book. Hsieh[13] narrates, "As she fought them, several tiny lights appeared to come from her mouth. Each time the light flashed … one of her opponents fell." Since the darts were not poisoned and quite tiny, she must have aimed at the eyes.

The blowing arrow is a lot longer but still small enough for multiple carries. Indeed, as many as six blowing arrows can be inserted into a bigger bamboo tube of the "plum blossom" type. I was unable to get a big bamboo tube for six blowing arrows but managed to get one where I was able to insert three (Figure 14-1).

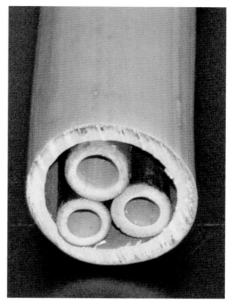

FIGURE 14-1. Three blowing arrows inserted in a bigger bamboo tube.

Each blowgun is loaded with a dart. The blowing arrows are inserted slightly staggered so that the shooter can bite one and pull it out with his teeth after which he shoots. After three shots, the shooter will have to fight with his empty hands.

There is a total lack of source material on how the Chinese masters of the past used the blowing arrow. However, I teach empty hands and weapons fighting and the following photographs illustrate how I would use the blowing arrow against two attackers (Figure 14-2).

Most other traditional blowguns are a lot longer than the blowing arrow. In the Philippines, where the zarbatana (sumpit) is at least 4 feet long, it is used as a staff when

- The shooter runs out of darts
- The blowgun might be already loaded with a dart but the attacker is too close.
- The attacker is ready to attack.

A number of commercial blowguns are designed to shoot darts as well as for use as walking canes or spears.

A whole book can be written on the use of the zarbatana as a staff. However, since this is a book on the use of the blowgun for shooting projectiles, only one sequence of defensive techniques will be illustrated in the use of the zarbatana as a weapon for striking.

Darts are sharp and are excellent for close quarter defense. Indeed, an attacker might not even be aware that his intended victim has one in his hand (Figure 14-4).

FIGURE 14-2. Using the blowgun against two attackers. The defender (Mat Jr.) right parries the knife thrust and hits the attacker's (Peter Sampogna) arm thereby deflecting it (A, B) then stabs the attacker on the throat with the blowgun (C). Mat Jr. keeps the attacker's arm in check and then elbows the attacker's biceps (D). He then aims and shoots the dart at the second attacker's (Fred Cupolo) throat (E).

A

B

C

D

E

A

B

C

FIGURE 14-3. Using the sumpit as a staff. As the attacker (Jose Capitulo) thrusts with a knife, the defender sidesteps to the left and hits the attacker's arm (A, B) with the sumpit then thrusts to the face (C).

FIGURE 15-1. The top four finishers at the First International Sport Blowgun Competition (left to right): Morikuni Matsumoto (1st), Dave Sustak (4th), Bruce Bell (3rd), Dr. Hironori Higuchi (2nd) (Photo courtesy of Bruce Bell).

chapter 16

TAKING CARE OF YOUR BLOWGUN

As a matter of good hygiene, wipe the mouthpiece of your blowgun with a wet towel before and after use.

You need to dry the inside of the barrel. Pull the cotton cloth through the barrel a couple of times before shooting the blowgun. After shooting, run water through the blowgun. Water from your breath left in the barrel could become host to harmful microorganisms.

It is not safe to lay down your blowgun on the floor. First of all, it can be accidentally stepped on. Secondly, it will eventually curve or warp. Do not lean a blowgun against a wall. If you have to put a thin-walled blowgun on the floor or lay it flat during transport, insert an uncut dowel in the bore of the blowgun. You need a dowel anyway in case a dart gets stuck in the bore.

FIGURE 16-1. Cleaning cloth hung from a tree branch can serve as wind direction and speed indicator.

To prevent my blowguns from curving, I hang them, by the quiver, on a blowgun rack that I designed (Figure 16-2). If your blowgun does not have a quiver, wrap duct tape a few inches from the breech and then you can hang it on the rack. Construct the rack with holes (openings) that will fit blowguns of different calibers.

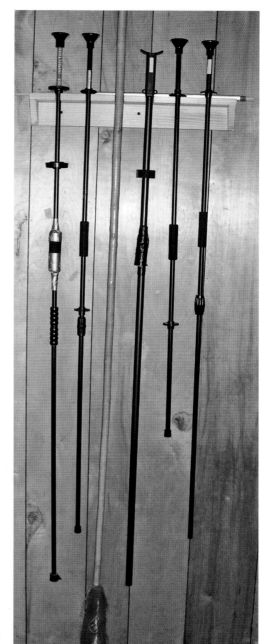

FIGURE 16-2. A rack I designed from which to hang my blowguns to prevent them from curving. I enlarged the opening on one to fit my tasseled spear (A, 3rd from left). Immediately to its right is a .625 caliber blowgun. All the others are .40 caliber blowguns. B shows the underside of the rack. (The rack was fabricated for me by my student Guro Ueli Laeng.)

A

B

chapter 17

THE ART OF
THE BLOWGUN

Up to the early 20th century, according to German and British thinkers, the key component of art was beauty.[9] Thus, if I were to justify the title of this chapter, I need to find "beauty" in the "art" of the blowgun.

Can we find "beauty" in the shooting of a blowgun? We can, but we need a lot of help from the ancients like Greek philosophers and from modern theorists and thinkers.

Plato[9] felt that beautiful objects incorporated proportion, harmony, and unity among their parts. Aristotle expounded that the universal elements of beauty were order, symmetry, and definiteness. They both referred to the beauty of the human physical form.

Theorists like William Hogarth[9] believes that "beauty consists of fitness of the parts to some design… and quantity or magnitude, which draws our attention and produces admiration and awe."

We can now find "beauty" in the "art" of the blowgun with their help. But first we have to break up the shooting of the blowgun into its parts: the act of shooting the blowgun, the flight of the dart, and the hitting of the target.

ACT OF SHOOTING THE BLOWGUN

The act of shooting the blowgun consists of

- Stance with blowgun by the hip
- Finger on cup to get dart
- Load
- Raise tip of blowgun toward target
- Push dart with thumb into the barrel
- Inhale, without removing the thumb
- Remove thumb
- Lower tip of blowgun to aim while holding breath
- Blow

Plato's notion of proportion is in reference to dimensional space. But time is also a dimension. Hence, if the time elapsed for each of the movements is not in proportion to the preceding or to the succeeding movement, there will be no harmony and no unity of movements. There will be no rhythm. If you take too much time to aim and if you inhale too much air the resulting shot will be "ugly."

FLIGHT OF THE DART

Beauty appeals to the senses visually as when we see Mona Lisa's smile or to the ears when we hear Mozart's music. However, we can hardly see the dart in its flight. Even if we can, it could not soar, glide, or fly like a bird for it has no mind of its own. However, it manifests mathematical beauty as is shown by the y equation and the presence of g. It may not be as elegant as $E=mc^2$ but at the time it was first derived, the y equation could have elicited a "Eureka!" And the g gives order to our universe. Mathematical beauty appeals to our sense of logic.

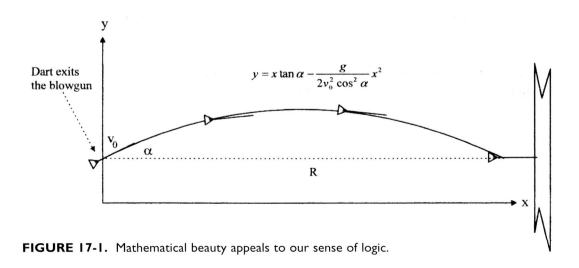

$$y = x \tan \alpha - \frac{g}{2v_0^2 \cos^2 \alpha} x^2$$

FIGURE 17-1. Mathematical beauty appeals to our sense of logic.

HITTING OF THE TARGET

I normally shoot only one dart at a given target. However, sometimes, I shoot as many as 10. In one instance, I shot 3 darts at one target. My first dart hit the bull's-eye. I shot two more darts but couldn't see where the darts hit from 33 feet. When I went to the target to retrieve the darts, I found one inside the other while the other hit its side!

One of the attributes of beauty, according to Hogarth is "quantity or magnitude which draws attention and produces admiration and awe." The 3 shots were a thing of "beauty."

FIGURE 17-2. Beauty draws attention and produces admiration and awe.

APPENDIX

APPENDIX A:
MEASURING THE VELOCITY OF A DART

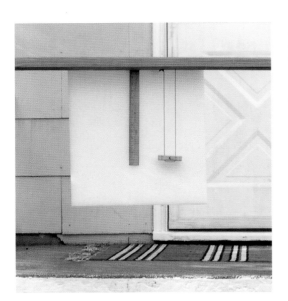

FIGURE 18A-1. The ballistic pendulum hanging from a 2 by 4 placed on top of a railing.

At first I considered buying a chronograph but then decided against it. Instead, I constructed a ballistic pendulum.

The ballistic pendulum is used to measure the velocity of a bullet. There is no reason why it cannot be used to measure the velocity of a dart.

The ballistic pendulum consists of a block of wood that is hung vertically with two cords. The dart is shot at the block of wood and becomes embedded in it. The wood swings upward and behaves like a pendulum.

I drilled two holes parallel to the edge of a 2 by 4 and then I threaded two cords attached to a 1 oz block of wood and placed the 2 by 4 on top of a railing just outside the door leading to my backyard (Figure 18A-1).

Since I would be measuring the height of the swing of the pendulum, I taped a ruler on a white foam background and focused a movie camera at the block of wood. I took the average of the height of the swing after shooting ten .50 caliber darts.

The formula for determining the velocity of the dart is

$$v_d = \frac{m_d + m_w}{m_d}(\sqrt{2gh})$$

(18A-1)

Here v_d is the velocity of the dart as it exits the muzzle, g is the gravitational constant and h is the height of the swing. The mass of the block of wood and dart are, respectively, m_w and m_d (Figure 18A-4).

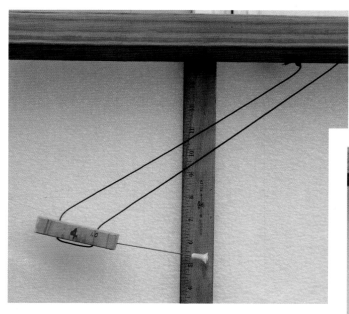

FIGURE 18A-2 (top). The ballistic pendulum after impact

FIGURE 18A-3 (right). The ballistic pendulum before impact

The masses of the dart and the wood can be determined using a scale while g is a constant. The height h of the swing can easily be measured. Hence, we can determine v_d the exit velocity of the dart. Substitute the values of md (0.03 oz), m_w (1.0 oz), g (32.2 ft/sec^2), and height of the swing of the wood block, h into equation (18A-1). My 10 shots using a .50 caliber blowgun gave me an average height of swing of 5.2 inches. Solving

$$v_d = \frac{0.03 + 1.0}{0.03}\sqrt{2(32.2)(\frac{5.2}{12})}$$

$$v_d = 181 ft/s \qquad (55 \text{ m/s})$$

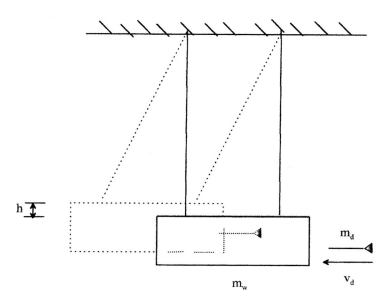

FIGURE 18A-4. Ballistic pendulum.[16] I placed the muzzle of the blowgun about two dart lengths away from the wood block to ensure that the air pushing the dart does not affect the swing of the pendulum.

Hence, the average velocity of my dart as it exits the blowgun is 181 ft/s (123 mph). Note that the mass units will cancel out, thus, it is not necessary to convert it to the proper units.

APPENDIX B: RULES OF COMPETITION

I. COMPETITION AREA. The space between the shooter and the target must be either 10 meters, 40 feet, or 50 feet. There must be 5 feet of free space to the left and to the right of the shooter.

A line will be drawn at the shooting distance parallel to the target boards.

No spectators will be allowed inside the competition area.

II. SHOOTING DISTANCE. 10 meters (32.8 feet), 40 feet, or 50 feet

III. SPECIFICATIONS OF BLOWGUNS AND DARTS.

LENGTH AND CALIBER OF BLOWGUN:

Distance	Length of blowgun	Caliber of blowgun
10 meters (32.8 feet)	at the most, 3' 5"	.40
40 meters	at the most, 4' 5"	.40
50 meters	at the most, 4' 5"	.40

LENGTH AND WEIGHT OF DART:

Length of dart	not more than 5"
Weight of dart	not more than 0.03 oz.

IV. THE TARGET.

HEIGHT OF THE TARGET: The center of the target should be 5 feet 6 inches from the ground.

SIZE AND POINTS OF THE TARGET:

Diameter of circle, inch	2	4	6	8
Points	5	4	3	1

V. DARTS TO BE SHOT.

NUMBER OF DARTS: 5 darts per round

NUMBER OF ROUNDS: 5 rounds

After each round, the scorer checks the darts and records the score, then the shooter can pull the darts off the target.

TOTAL NUMBER OF DARTS TO BE SHOT: 25

VI. TIME TO SHOOT: 5 minutes per round

VII. SCORING:

When the dart hits the line of the circle, it is scored the higher point. For example: If the dart hits the line of the circle between the 4 inch and the 2 inch diameter circles, the dart is scored 5 points.

VIII. IN CASE OF A TIE:

The competitor who has the most number of hits inside the 2 inch diameter circle will be declared the winner.

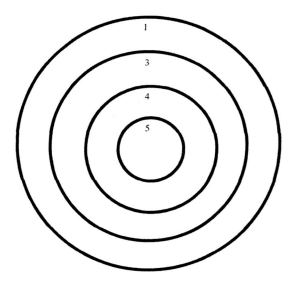

FIGURE 18B-1.

APPENDIX C: COMPETITION SCORE SHEET

Target, circles	Round:		
	Number of sticks	Points	Total
Inside 2"		5	
4"		4	
6"		3	
8"		1	
Outside 8"		0	
Total			

APPENDIX D:
RECORD SHEET FOR EACH SET OF 10 DARTS

Target, circles	10	20	30	40	50	60	70	80	90	100	Total
Inside 2"											
4"											
6"											
8"											
Outside 8"											
A drop											
Total	10	10	10	10	10	10	10	10	10	10	100

APPENDIX E:
SUMMARY SHEET FOR EACH SET OF 100 DARTS

Target, circles	100 darts			100 darts		
	Number of sticks	Points	Total	Number of sticks	Points	Total
Inside 2"		5			5	
4"		4			4	
6"		3			3	
8"		1			1	
Outside 8"		0	0		0	0
A drop		0	0		0	0
Total						

APPENDIX F:
MONTHLY SUMMARY OF TOTAL POINTS AVERAGE

Distance: _____ Length of blowgun: _____ Weight/length of dart: _____

Date	Jan	Feb	Mar	Apr	May	Jun	Jul	Aug	Sep	Oct	Nov	Dec
1												
2												
3												
4												
5												
6												
7												
8												
9												
10												
11												
12												
13												
14												
15												
16												
17												
18												
19												
20												
21												
22												
23												
24												
25												
26												
27												
28												
29												
30												
31												
Total points average												
Total points per dart												

Note: Average points per dart = Total points average/100

This formula applies only if you shoot 100 darts each day.

APPENDIX G: YEARLY SUMMARY FOR CONSECUTIVE MONTHS

Month	Total points average	Average points per dart
January		
February		
March		
April		
May		
June		
July		
August		
September		
October		
November		
December		

12-MONTH SUMMARY FOR NON-CONSECUTIVE MONTHS

Month Number	Total points average	Average points per dart
1		
2		
3		
4		
5		
6		
7		
8		
9		
10		
11		
12		

APPENDIX H: SAMPLE CALCULATIONS

You can track your progress by keeping a log of your hits and misses in a shooting session. Using Table H-1, Table H-2, and Table H-3 you can create Table H-4. You can generate Figure H-1 from Table H-4.

TABLE H-1. Points assigned to each dart.

Diameter of circle, inch	2	4	6	8
Points	5	4	3	1

TABLE H-2. Six-day shooting log.

	Monday	Tuesday	Wednesday	Thursday	Friday	Saturday	Total
Inside 2"	14	21	14	21	16	21	107
Inside 4"	36	29	40	33	37	34	209
Inside 6"	36	33	34	33	33	34	203
Inside 8"	14	17	12	13	14	11	81
Total	100	100	100	100	100	100	600

TABLE H-3. Daily Total Points.

Monday	No. of darts	Points	Total points
Inside 2"	14	5	70
Inside 4"	36	4	144
Inside 6"	36	3	108
Inside 8"	14	1	14
Total	100		336

Thursday	No. of darts	Points	Total points
Inside 2"	21	5	105
Inside 4"	33	4	132
Inside 6"	33	3	99
Inside 8"	13	1	13
Total	100		349

Tuesday	No. of darts	Points	Total points
Inside 2"	21	5	105
Inside 4"	29	4	116
Inside 6"	33	3	99
Inside 8"	17	1	17
Total	100		337

Friday	No. of darts	Points	Total points
Inside 2"	16	5	80
Inside 4"	37	4	148
Inside 6"	33	3	99
Inside 8"	14	1	14
Total	100		341

Wednesday	No. of darts	Points	Total points
Inside 2"	14	5	70
Inside 4"	40	4	160
Inside 6"	34	3	102
Inside 8"	12	1	12
Total	100		344

Saturday	No. of darts	Points	Total points
Inside 2"	21	5	105
Inside 4"	34	4	136
Inside 6"	34	3	102
Inside 8"	11	1	11
Total	100		354

TABLE H-4. Values plotted in Figure H-1.

	Total points	Average*
Monday	336	3.36
Tuesday	337	3.37
Wednesday	344	3.44
Thursday	349	3.49
Friday	341	3.41
Saturday	354	3.54
Average* = Total points/100 darts		

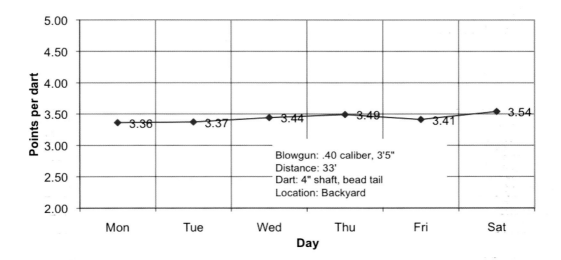

FIGURE H-1. A line graph of the average points per bead dart as shown in Table H-4.

END NOTES

1. D. M. da Silva, Sao Paulo, Brazil, personal communications
2. Q-tip is a trade name owned by Unilever
3. J. Man & The Editors of Time-Life Books, *Jungle Nomads of Ecuador: The Waorani*, (Time-Life Books, Amsterdam, 1982)
4. M. D. Janich, *Blowguns: The Breath of Death*, (Paladin Press, Boulder, Colorado, 1993)
5. C. Toops, *Hummingbirds: Jewels in Flight*, (Voyageur Press, Inc., Stillwater, Minnesota, 1982)
6. J.D. Walker, Karate Strikes, *American Journal of Physics* 43, 845, 1975
7. H. Blum, *American Journal of Physics* 45, 61-64, 1977
8. C. Soo, *The Chinese Art of K'ai Men*, (Gordon and Cremonesi Publishers, London & New York, 1977)
9. Wikepedia, The Free Encyclopedia, 2008
10. L. J. Goldstein, D. C. Lay, and D. I. Schneider, (*Mathematics for the Management, Life and Social Sciences*, Prentice-Hall Inc., Englewood Cliffs, NJ, 1984)
11. D. L. Stancel and M. L. Stancel, *Applications of College Mathematics*, (D.C. Heath and Company, Massachusetts, 1983)
12. P. Descola, *The Spears of Twilight: Life and Death in the Amazon Jungle*, (The New Press, New York, New York, 1996)
13. L. Becker, *Adventures with the Blowgun*, (The Backwoodsman, Volume 28, No. 5, Sept/Oct 2007, Los Alamos, New Mexico)
14. D. H. Y. Hsieh, *Ancient Chinese Weapons*, (Meadea Enterprise Co., Inc., Republic of China, 1986)
15. Mainichi Daily News, (November 25, 2007)
16. E. L. Little, *The Audubon Society Field Guide to North American Trees*, (Alfred A. Knopf, Inc., New York, New York, 1980)
17. F. Sears, *University Physics*, (Addison-Wesley, New Jersey, 1976)

Other texts referenced:

P. Brancazio, *Sport Science*, (Simon & Schuster, 1984, New York, New York)

M. S. Feld, R. E. McNair and S.R. Wilk, *American Journal of Physics* 51, 783-790, 1983

A. van Heuvelen, *Physics a General Introduction*, (Little, Brown and Company, Boston, Toronto, 1986)

D. C. Giancoli, *Physics Principles with Applications*, (Prentice-Hall, Inc., Englewood Cliffs, NJ, 1985)

D. Haliday, and R. Resnick, *Fundamentals of Physics*, (John Wiley & Sons, 1970)

P. G. Hewitt, *Conceptual Physics*, (Little, Brown and Company, Boston, Toronto, 1985)

H. Higuchi, personal communication, IFA website

A. P. Mariñas, *Pananandata Guide to Sport Blowguns*, (United Cutlery Corporation, Sevierville, Tennessee, 1999)

P. J. Ouseph, *Technical Physics*, (D. Van Nostrand Company, New York, New York, 1980)

P. Hougham, *Encyclopedia of Archery*, (Barnes, New York, 1958)

Note: I read (10) about 20 years ago and I cannot remember who to give credit to for Equations (7-1) and (12-1)—my apologies to the authors. I read both books at the Elmhurst Public Library when I was still living in Queens, New York and I have lived in Fredericksburg, Virginia since July 1997.